PROSTATE IN THE SUN

KEN ROBSON

prostate in the sun

STOLL PUBLISHING
2001

First edition published in 2001 by
Stoll Publishing
25 Richmond Way
London W14 0AS

Copyright © Ken Robson 2001
Cover illustration by the author

ISBN 0 9539568-0-6

A catalogue record for this book is available from the British Library

Ken Robson's right to be identified as the author of this work has been asserted by him in accordance with the Copyright, Designs and Patents Act 1988

Typeset in New Century 12/13pt
by Scriptmate Editions

Manufacture coordinated in UK by Book-in-Hand Ltd,
20 Shepherds Hill, London N6 5AH

All rights reserved. No part of this book may be reproduced or transmitted in any form, electronic or mechanical, including photocopy or any information storage and retrieval system, without permission in writing from the publisher.

Foreword

It is with enormous pleasure that I write this introduction to the story of one man's battle with his prostate.

For many years male cancers have been something of a cinderella in the world of Oncology. Some men find it extremely difficult to discuss health issues and especially diseases such as prostate cancer with all the implications concerning virility.

There has recently been an information revolution with extensive and detailed facts concerning prostate cancer in the media, on television and of course on the Internet. This is a welcome change and at last prostate cancer is receiving the attention it deserves with regard to diagnosis and treatment. However sometimes these facts can be confusing, and from my experience working with patients at all stages of this disease, many feel extremely lonely around the time of diagnosis and have difficulty sharing basics concerns with family and friends.

In his book Ken has recorded his own feelings at each stage of his journey with prostate cancer. He has described the investigations and treatment with accuracy and more importantly has added insight, touching honesty and always a sense of humour. For many men who have been diagnosed with 'prostate problems' or prostate cancer, in these pages they will find someone who has been there and who understands. I am sure that reading these pages will help to remove some of the isolation at such a difficult time.

I think that this is also an excellent book for all of us who are involved in the treatment of prostate disease. It gives the most amazing insight into the most important factor in treating prostate cancer, that is the patient himself.

Dr H A Payne
Consultant Clinical Oncologist
The Meyerstein Institute of Oncology, London

FIONA

To list individually all those who have helped me in completing this book, and to whom I am indebted — in some form or another — would maybe risk upsetting the one who I am sure I would inadvertently omit or maybe several of those whom I would deliberately include. To all of you my most heartfelt thanks.

CHAPTER ONE

It was in the early seventies. We were sitting at my mother's large kitchen table at one of those all too infrequent, but nevertheless enjoyable, informal family gatherings. At the corner of the table sat an elderly uncle, a widower. He had been a massive man in his youth with hands like the proverbial York Hams but by nature as gentle as a lamb. He had been a shepherd all his life.

During the course of the meal he had to get up and leave the table so many times and not without some difficulty, which made his leaving more apparent, that my mother was forced to whisper in very hallowed tones, "He has a problem with his water works. Prostate, you know, and he won't go to the doctor." No, we didn't know but nobody asked and another topic of conversation quickly covered the silence.

That was the first and only time in my life, up to that day, and indeed for more than two decades to come, that I ever heard the word 'prostate' mentioned in any conversation.

It was in the early nineties that I first began to notice that I was getting up more times than normal during the course of the night, to go for a 'pee'. I was then in my late fifties and in pretty good shape physically; swimming mostly every day, eating sensibly, being fed the right amount of tablets and capsules that contain all the good things that your body needs to stay healthy, but, so I am informed, may not necessarily be in the foods we consume in this day and age — no matter how 'organic' we may think we are.

I put my extra nocturnal trips down to drinking a little more than usual and my body slowing down. After all, like it or not, I was not getting any younger. Such typical male thinking. We are so good at making excuses for ourselves, at self-deception, especially when it comes to anything affecting our bodies, or more especially, certain parts of our bodies. Of course I hadn't increased my intake of drink. I ran a bar-restaurant and by habit I drank about the same amount every day, maybe too much in some people's eyes, but about the same. In fact on reflection, maybe I was drinking less. I had long since given up imbibing gin or whiskey, preferring the delights of wine or cold beer. Being aware that my waist line was thickening, I was as equally aware of the 'beer belly' profile and there was no way I was going to allow one of those to flop over my belt, so I was cutting down on the lagers too.

I was also doing the Leslie Kenton ten day Detox Diet at least twice a year. At the end of which you feel so great you wonder why you ever take another drink or visit a burger-bar ever again.

So who was kidding who? I was still getting up during the night, more times than I should. My macho ego would not allow me to consider that there was anything amiss with my 'water-works'. They were fine. 'There was nothing wrong with my 'willy'.

My new nocturnal habit continued, it didn't get noticeably worse, it certainly did not get better. I continued quite deliberately to ignore it.

After a time I began to notice another unusual occurrence creeping into my daily habits. Busting for a 'pee' I would rush into the 'loo', stand in front of the urinal; let out a long relieving 'Aaaaah' but no long relieving 'pee'. OK, relax, let out a long deep breath, give 'willy' a couple of encouraging shakes and... at last. The relief...

Looking back I cannot recall the exact time span over which these symptoms manifested themselves. I was desperately trying to ignore the whole thing — I continued to convince myself that I had no problem. At the same time, I never breathed a word of it to anyone else. Heaven forbid!

In common with most males I was at that time — I am not so bad now — very reluctant to read the label on a box of pills let alone visit a doctor. I was living in the Canaries, that group of small islands nestling in the Atlantic Ocean off the coast of Morocco. They are blessed with a climate that some consider to be the best in the world. All year round summer, no humidity, a cooling breeze, champagne air and if there is any pollution in the sea it is very difficult to find.

I recall lying on the little beach in the old town of Puerto del Carmen on Lanzarote, it was a Christmas day, sometime in the middle eighties, when a friend of mine came dripping out of the sea, threw himself on his towel and declared, "You've just got to do this for the rest of your life. Prostrate in the sun."

I was half-asleep. "What was that you said?"

"You know. Lying here, rest of your natural. Prostrate in the sun."

"Oh, I thought you said something else."

My mind leapt back to lunches round a big kitchen table... I thought I had heard that word once again. Little did I know how many times it was to come up...

The doctors in the Canaries are of course, Spanish. Never having had the need of their services up until that time, my knowledge of Spanish medical terms was zilch and I was not quite sure, that with my conversational Spanish, I could adequately explain my problem. "No puedo pasar mi aqua." Translated 'I cannot pass my water' — while standing in front of a doctor waving my hand in front of my fly did not seem enough!

All this, of course, added up to the delay in doing something about it. But my newly acquired personal habits were not going to go away and as I was not entirely bereft of grey matter I knew I HAD to do something, however many excuses I could contrive.

Another party eventually convinced me to go to a private practice where they spoke English. Now, why hadn't I thought of that? Why? Because I wasn't ready to face the truth, was I? Although we men don't talk about it, I was aware in my sub-conscious, that if you have problems with… er… you know what — which, without doubt, I had — then there are things that lie in store for you that are so totally unacceptable that you cannot find the words to describe them, and you certainly did not want to hear them. But inwardly I knew going to an English-speaking doctor was a good idea. I would think about it.

The appointment was made for me.

CHAPTER TWO

The Norwegian doctor spoke English. In fact he spoke better English than I did, well maybe not better, but a lot better than the English spoken by some that I know. Why is it that apparently, all Norwegians speak such good English when I do not know one Englishman who speaks good Norwegian? I was once told by a chappie from Lurgen, which I think is somewhere up in the Arctic circle, that there were so few of them that unless they spoke English they could never find anyone to talk to.

I sat in front of him — the Norwegian doctor that is, not the chappie from Lurgan — and explained all that had been happening to me. It was the first time I had spoken about it to a stranger. But then we don't look upon doctors as strangers, do we. It was just the first time I had spoken to anyone.

He listened carefully, encouraging me with his silence to waffle on. Doctors do that, sit there knowingly, appraising. I paused. He stopped tapping the ends of his fingers together in front of his jaw, took his elbows off the armrests, leaned forward on his desk and said, "It sounds very much like you have a prostate problem."

"Oh, really," said I, a little too quickly, almost butting in, but casually, as if it were something that came up in any everyday conversation.

Of course I had a prostate problem, for God's sake! I had sub-consciously known that I had a prostate problem for months. What I didn't understand is why the only time we hear the word prostate it has to come from a doctor which, for a lot of men, may be far too late. We all seem to be aware of the word but no one ever uses it. Not even in the privacy of our own families!

There is a phrase "Don't mention the war". Now that is the phrase that should not be used. The 'war' decimated the male population of the United Kingdom. The prostate problem affects one male in every three. At the present time, each year, some ten thousand men die from cancer of the prostate. It is the second biggest 'killer disease' of men in the UK and we don't talk about it! As a society, both socially and politically we ignore it. The money spent on research into the problem in a year would barely cover six months' wages of one of our 'prima donna' Premiership footballers.

We have no awareness of the problem therefore we can take no steps to avoid the problem. I reached the age of fifty-eight and only became aware that I had a PROSTATE problem because I had it! Talk about 'Don't mention the pros...prost... you know the water-work thing.'

My Norwegian doctor then carried out a physical examination. He asked me to drop my trousers and underpants, lie on the couch on my side, and face the wall. The wall looked cold, bare, stark white, uninviting; still my fingers ran over its surface seeking reassurance. A feeling of being very alone swept over me. The snap of the rubber gloves echoed around the room. Acute trepidation was immediate.

This turned out to be quite unwarranted, as the physical examination is totally pain free. In fact, one could say, though, of course I never would, that there is a certain amount of pleasure attached to it. A finger, concealed in rubber glove, is inserted into the anus with which the size and texture of the prostate gland can be assessed and a prognosis given. The 'Doc' advised me that I had a benign enlargement of the prostate.

Now should you be unfortunate enough to become the one in the 'one-in-three' males that become inflicted with this common-or-garden complaint, you will find yourself submitting to this examination on a regular basis. In fact I have got so used to it that, even if I am only visiting a hospital or doctor's surgery or even if I get just a whiff of disinfectant, I have this sudden compulsion to drop my trousers and look for a couch to lie on and face the wall. Maybe it is the pleasurable exper… Naah!

The doctor gave me a brief explanation of my symptoms, told me it was a matter for a specialist consultant and gave me a letter of introduction to an urologist, that is someone who specialises in 'water-work' problems, at the local hospital.

I believe it was at this point that I finally acknowledged that I had a prostate gland, that I had a prostate problem, and I actually accepted the word into my vocabulary.

But what is a prostate gland? Put, as I understand it and in layman's terms, it is a gland that produces or secretes the fluid in which the semen travels. It is located at the very lowest part of your body below your bladder and between your anus and your scrotum. Its normal size is that of a walnut and it should feel smooth to touch. Through the centre of it passes a tube through which you pass all the fluids that you discharge from your body via your 'willy'. When the gland gets enlarged it compresses on the tube and you get a 'problem' — a restricted flow.

Apart from the physical examination, the condition and more specifically the activity of the gland can be measured by another fluid that it secretes into the bloodstream, known as the Prostate Specific Antigen, the PSA reading. So every time you have a check up you have to have a blood test.

My first visit to the urologist, Mr Martinez, took place in his consulting rooms in Arrecife, the island capital. I took to him straight away. He had a sympathetic yet confident manner that came at you in a positive friendly way, he showed that he cared, a trait developed by all good practitioners.

He referred to the letter of introduction, I explained my problems and he gave me the customary examination. I lay down; again the snap of the rubber gloves made me stiffen. Relax. His diagnosis confirmed that I did indeed have a benign enlargement of the prostate.

I was also, in his opinion, somewhat on the young side to have such a problem and therefore considered that the best treatment for me would be to have the now relatively straightforward prostatetectomy, an operation that removes the unwanted swollen tissue pressing against the urethra, the tube. This is achieved, in simple terms, by sticking a highly technical complicated metal rod, called a resectoscope up your 'willy', and either by means of an electrical current or a blade, scouring out the enlarged tissue much as you would de-core an apple. Baked apples will never be the same again.

Although one gets no noticeable scars, and no major wall of the body is cut it is still regarded as a major operation and you may require up to one week's convalescence in hospital, as well as taking things easy for a couple of months afterwards.

Mr Martinez then explained the possible, repeat possible, side-effects that may arise — or may not arise — as the case maybe.

Now believe me this is where, if you cannot avoid the operation, not only is your fate in the skilful hands of your surgeon but also in the hands of 'Lady Luck', or whoever else you may call on in your hour of need. Because the 'weapons of beneficial destruction' used in the operation come perilously close to the minuscule intricate nerve endings that control an awful lot of your natural day-to-day functions.

I have always maintained that every emission from the body is a pleasure and the area of the prostate is desperately close to a number of such pleasures.

So here then are a few of the side-effects that can occur although I would emphasise that with the ever-increasing medical computer technology your chances of suffering from them are receding.

Incontinence — you are unable to control your 'pee', you may have to wear a drain bag, or if you dribble a bit, a nappy. Retrograde ejaculation — meaning quite simply that instead of your 10cc of semen shooting out of the end of your 'willy' it shoots into your bladder, which you discharge when next you 'pee' — and no, you don't get the pleasure all over again. It may be stating the obvious, but if it is your intention to add to this already crowded planet, then, prior to the operation you should hedge your bets by putting a sizeable deposit in a local 'Sperm Bank'. You'll find them in the Yellow Pages.

Impotency. There it is. I'll say it again IMPOTENCY. The big one. In simple terms it means... it means... We all know what it means, that is why we don't talk about it. It means. 'You can't get it up!' No wonder that little voice inside me keeps screaming 'There's nothing wrong with my 'willy'. It is unimaginable. It cannot happen.

I am loathe to quote odds or statistics, as they can always be manipulated and changed to suit conditions, but what are the considered chances of suffering any of these consequences? Incontinence is now quite rare—thank God for that—and the dreaded impotence occurs in twenty to thirty men in every hundred. Yes a twenty to thirty per cent chance. Retrograde ejaculation is the odd one out. It is a generally held view that if you undergo this operation this condition will occur. But it doesn't. Not always and there doesn't seem to be an explanation. You are also advised that should it occur you should not consider yourself to be in a safe sex situation. Contraception is still recommended.

Mr Martinez explained all these possibilities in a positive, shall I say light-hearted manner, well he must repeat them so often with every third man he passes in the street either a customer or a potential customer. He advised me that my PSA reading, taken from a blood sample I had given earlier, was at the higher end of what you would call normal. The pills, prescribed for me by my Norwegian doctor were easing the difficulty to 'pee' and so there was no rush to make an immediate decision. Think about it, he prompted and come back and see me within three months.

Think about it. I wanted to think that it wasn't happening to me. This only happens to old men, men like my uncle, in his eighties.

I did not have to think about it for long. My mind was to be made up for me.

CHAPTER THREE

The restaurant that I ran was in the old part of Puerto del Carmen, above the harbour and it was my custom to open the bar, on my own, about an hour or so before the staff came on. It was a part of the day that I really enjoyed, catching the sunburnt faces of the latest arrivals — old and new — coming off the beach, looking to quench their thirst; and those residents who preferred to drink at the beginning of the evening, rather than later, 'early-doors' they called it. Usually it was not too busy, allowing me to enact the full part of Mine Host to the best of my ability — a welcome here, a short conversation there and there, the best one liners I could think of, informatively using my local knowledge to tell people where to go and what to do and of course, fervently listening to or helping to dispense the local gossip. For a short while each day I was, so to speak, centre stage, and I enjoyed it.

One evening, not long after I had seen the specialist, (I was still thinking about it) as I was opening up I noticed a few people waiting outside. A good sign I thought, the promise of a good evening's trade. Nothing wrong with that. I got into my act. Serving drinks as quickly as I could. The bar was buzzing.

I then began to feel the first signs of wanting to 'pee'. More people came in. This was unusual, I think one of the larger tour operators must have put my name on their 'places to visit' list. My 'signs' became a desire. Practically every one of my 'early-doors' must have come in. I served and tried to keep my cool, to play the part. My 'desire' became urgent with a capital 'U'. I got to the stage of literally 'busting for a pee'. With a half muttered 'Excuse me' I dashed to the 'loo'.

Now this was, if ever there was, a time when you did not want any difficulties, but Sod's Law prevailed. Could I go? I must have been in there seven or eight minutes — it seemed like a year.

I had been in there so long that I really wished that everybody had left. 'Sod the cash in the till'. The 'loos' were situated at the end of the bar, up two fairly high steps, so when you returned to the bar you could not help but make some sort of entrance — you could go all theatrical, if you wanted, many people did. Me, that night, I just wanted to slither, unnoticed, round the corner. No chance. Everyone had stayed and more had come in, they were two deep at the bar — waiting to be served. All eyes were on me. They must have known where I'd been — they couldn't help but know where I had been. Up there, there was no other place to go.

My embarrassment was massive. I even imagined I heard someone whisper in very hallowed tones "He's got a problem with his water-works. You know ...". Yes I knew, but I had, unlike many other sufferers, been to the doctor and I was going again. This was the moment my mind was made up. I was not going to go through this, or anything similar ever again. I was going to get 'sorted'. One way or another. I was going to have the operation.

I obtained an appointment with the urologist Mr Martinez fairly quickly. My PSA reading had risen slightly and he agreed with my decision. There would be a delay of about four to five weeks before I could be admitted to hospital, had I have been paying privately I could have gone in that day. 'It's the same the whole world over'. Well almost that day, there were one or two tests and an X-ray to be taken before the operation. For these my bladder had to be empty and my bowels 'vacated' — as he put it.

He wrote out a prescription for the powder and equipment necessary to perform the enema and instructed me that on the day of the tests I should neither eat nor drink and carry out the enema process three times, at hourly intervals, prior to the visit.

'Enemas' — three times — on my own! I was moving into the world of the seriously unknown here. The only experience I had of enemas was in a jocular sense from the 'Carry on Nurse' film and that somewhat slick, if not sick, one-liner 'If God wanted to give the world an enema he would stick the tube in …' and you provide whatever word you wish.

Mr Martinez advised me that following the instructions carefully, and with the help of a partner, or even on my own, it was a relatively simple operation. I left his office with a piece of white paper in my hand — the prescription — and some trepidation in my heart. I had taken the first steps down the road to…

The day of the tests arrived. 'The love of my life' was out, working, quite deliberately I believe, as when we had briefly discussed the matter her words were something like "I think I'll leave this one to you". So I was on my own. I had read the instructions several times and was feeling quite confident; after all I have always been a bit of a handy man around the house, the odd little maintenance job was never a problem and what was this — just a bit of simple plumbing really.

The kit consisted of several packets of powder, which had to be mixed with tepid water, a plastic tube with a tap and a nozzle at one end and a plastic bag at the other that would hold the tepid mixture. The whole lot then to be suspended from a point that was, obviously, higher than the point of entry.

Having considered the types of accidents that could possibly, or more probably occur, I chose the bathroom as my operating theatre; tiled floor and walls, toilet and bidet nearby and immediate access to running water in the bath and shower. The carpet and cushions on the centre of the living room floor were considered, but not for long.

I made my preparations and put a large towel on the bathroom floor on which I would lie — on my side, facing the wall, of course. I hung the bag of liquid on the shower curtain rail only to find that the plastic nozzle did not reach the point of entry when I lay on the floor. The instructions were quite explicit; I had to be lying down. I looked around. There was nowhere else it could hang. Mmmm, I should have done a dummy run, I told myself. How do I get over this?

Well, what would the whole of modern civilisation do without the multi-purpose, time saving, self-propagating wire coat hanger that is always there in every wardrobe on the planet? Its contributions to the quality of life are so enormous it would take a week to list them. I quickly fashioned two of them into a hook and thus lowered the bag containing the liquid. I lay down and inserted the nozzle — KY is a wonderful product. I gingerly turned on the tap — ahem — a strange feeling, again not unpleasant. I lay very still, I was supposed to allow the container to empty, which I managed and retain the fluid inside me for as long as possible. I clenched the buttocks tight — the lavatory pan beckoned — no, I must retain it as long as possible. Getting up was not easy. I clenched my teeth as well, hard. I was hypnotised by the lavatory pan. I had to pull myself away. I tried a few steps around the apartment, not a good idea. Back to the bathroom —rapidly. It was then that I learnt the truth in that old adage 'What goes up must come down'.

I managed to repeat the exercise as ordered — practice makes perfect. There were no major mishaps and I ended up strangely light-headed, with an empty feeling in the pit of my stomach and a strong feeling of self-satisfaction of having achieved something.

I have since discovered that the whole process is said to have therapeutic benefits and is available, at a price, in several up-market Health clubs under the grandiose title of 'Colonic Irrigation'. I'm sorry but that sounds like a load of 'crap' to me.

I went directly to the hospital where the tests and X-rays were carried out and after a couple of days I arrived back in the office of Mr Martinez. He advised me that everything had gone according to plan, there were no signs of any further complications and arranged a date for me to be admitted to hospital.

CHAPTER FOUR

The hospital had only been opened a year or so. It had that clean-cut modern look, glaringly white. Two storeys high, built around attractive garden squares. And on the first and second floors there were covered terraces outside allowing the patients to sit or stroll in the ideal climate of the Canaries.

The reception hall was vast. The marbled floor, the walls of volcanic rock and the indoor gardens were impressive, but hardly friendly. I recalled the first hospital that I had cause to visit. It was shortly after I had, at the tender age of six, put my equally tender hand, SMACK straight on the face of my mother's hot iron. We walked to the hospital, at least my mother did, I was carried, howling. It was called The Hendon Cottage Hospital. Cottage was the important word; many hospitals in those days had 'Cottage' included in their title. It is a nice word, rustic, homely, suggesting loving tenderness and care. Aaaah. A long way from the clinical startling white look of today.

We arrived at 7.45pm for an 8pm admission. We pushed open the heavy glass doors and with an air of completely unnatural confidence, we stepped across the deserted hall towards a sign that said receptionist. We presented ourselves and were advised in an extremely positive manner that we were not expected until 10pm! I had never really believed that we had the time right at as late as 8pm, let alone 10. This could never have occurred in a 'Cottage' hospital.

For some unknown reason I had not eaten since mid-day and had been advised that there was no food available in the hospital after 8pm. I repaired to the nearby cafeteria and ordered a coffee and a cheese and ham roll. It was all they had — the cafeteria closed at 8.

'The love of my life' was into some quite heavy negotiations with the receptionist who finally ascertained that we could go up to the ward.

The lift floated us to the second floor in an unearthly silence. We walked out into an equally silent corridor. Which way? A nurse glided round a corner and led us to room 205.

In common with most recently built hospitals the wards here were split into small rooms with provision for one, two or four patients. This was a small room with two beds, four chairs, two bedside lockers, a dual wardrobe, a television set and an en suite bathroom. The bathroom had all the regular fittings, a shower not a bath and an exception, not so obvious to the British eye, no bidet. Surprising in a newly built hospital on the continent.

The other bed was filled with a large thickset native to the island, whom the nurse introduced as Carlos. Carlos spoke no English but had a passionate love for 'Lucha' wrestling, as do the majority of Canarians. This is a truly amateur sport, one of the few that are left — for men only as yet — and I mean big strapping fellows of various weights, who attempt to pull each other's shorts off — well that's what it looks like to the uninitiated and the winner is the one left standing. Such is the passion for this sport that each town in the Canaries, be it big or small, has its own Lucha Stadium; complete with car park, sand-filled ring, tiered seating and they compete in a seasonal league. It is very competitive.

If you happen to be the biggest and heaviest of them all and you consistently beat all you meet, then you are given the much sort-after title 'El Pollo' — which literally translated means 'The Chicken'. A different culture — a different interpretation. Carlos was passionate about his 'Lucha' as his sport, to the exclusion of all others, as I was to find out.

My Spanish was good enough to communicate with Carlos on most things, so long as they were not medical. I never did get to learn what he was in for — I felt it was a bit like, I believe, the unwritten law in prison 'You don't ask'. In the long run he turned out to be a good companion.

'The love of my...' saw me settled in and left me with kisses, a big hug and the best of luck for tomorrow. I settled down with the previous day's paper, I was looking forward to an early night.

At 9.15pm there entered a nurse carrying a tray, which she put on the table over the end of the bed and pushed it towards me. I sat up, somewhat apprehensively and lifted the lid. There on a tray, three times as big as the one you get on an airplane, was a full sized meal.

At this point some doubts began to creep... no leap into my mind. An 8pm admission that should have been 10, no food after 8 and I get a meal at 9.15... I might have to keep a wary eye open.

The meal consisted of soup, an omelette, side salad, two halves of a tinned peach in juice and two packets of hard toast, which I put on one side. I tried the omelette and ate the peaches. Replacing the cover, I pushed the table to the end of the bed and returned to my paper.

A little while later, just as I was dropping off, the nurse returned with a sleeping pill. Yes I had to take it. I lay awake for some time contemplating the coming day. I wished the pill would work. It di...

CHAPTER FIVE

Up to this point I have been in nine different hospitals, all for a variety of reasons, none of which were life threatening. They read like a list of personal attainments — in fact, apart from a few O levels — they are my only personal attainments — Hendon Cottage, Edgeware General (twice), Barnet General, British Military Hamburg, North Middlesex, St Charles Ladbrook Grove, The Middlesex and the Insulad General Lanzarote. I've just remembered a tenth, I had my tonsils out in a hospital in Enfield, near the Ridgeway, but I cannot remember its name. I have thought that I might abbreviate them to initials and add them all to my CV, that's if I ever have reason to need another CV.

Over the years, the hospital experience that I have had probably makes me far more ultra-receptive and therefore more ultra-critical than say, a first time patient. A 'been there, seen it, done it all before' attitude and probably a pain in the 'butt' to all hospital staff.

A new experience awaited me the following morning. I was awoken at 8.30am, a very reasonable, if not an unbelievably late hour for most hospitals. The nurse took my temperature, blood pressure and hung a notice above my bed, which translated quite simply as STARVE. A bit to the point, I thought. She was closely followed by a short, crew-cut grey haired male nurse dressed in a green uniform, wearing thick horn-rimmed spectacles and with a very military bearing. He carried in his rubber-gloved hands, a metal kidney shaped bowl, which contained, as far as I could see, an open blade razor. A collector's piece! I cowered under the sheet. He's not coming near me with that.

"Operacion," he barked, apparently to anyone who was listening. Carlos said nothing, he was still asleep. I was just wondering if I should own up, when the nurse noticed the sign above my bed and, surprisingly, turned on his heel with precision and marched out of the room.

I breathed a sigh of relief; the thought of that open-razor in front of those horn-rimmed glasses hovering over my 'privates' did not bear contemplating. To be shorn of any of one's body hair makes one feel so uncomfortably naked and vulnerable. Was I beginning to feel nervous?

A nurse came with breakfast for Carlos, who had now condescended to join us. She ordered me to shower, shave — chin that is — do what else was necessary and to get back into bed naked. This I did at a leisurely pace and continued reading my paper. After reading the same paragraph several times and not getting even a smile out the cartoon page I knew I was just pretending.

For the last couple of weeks I had striven, quite successfully, to keep the forthcoming events of this particular day out of my mind. Now the decision had been made there was no going back, all I could do was go along with it in a positive frame of mind, believing that everything would go according to plan. My other hospital experiences helped a lot. I had been through this so many times before and seen so many others go through such a day.

At the same time I was reminded that I must let the anaesthetist know that I had been subjected to anaesthetics some fourteen times previously. Evidently you can build up a sort of immunity so it takes longer to 'put you under'. I had found this out, when after my last operation several years before, when the anaesthetist had come to check me out, after I had 'come round'. He explained that after the anaesthetic if you start counting backwards from a hundred you should normally drop off before you get to ninety. It was when I had got to seventy-nine seventy-eight… that he began to get fidgety.

When it got to about mid-day, I was thinking to myself that at least I was not the first one on the slab to-day — by the time I got down there they should all be well warmed up and have their eye in.

Then at last my green-suited, short little man re-appeared. In a very practised, efficient manoeuvre, and showing a strength that was far from obvious, he soon had me sailing down the corridor, but not before Carlos had given me the traditional international thumbs up and a cheery "Good luck".

On all my previous visits to the theatre I had always had the 'pre-med' in the ward, and when heaved on to a trolley, had floated down the corridors on cloud nine, with a stupid grin on my face and humming 'Here we go again…'. In this hospital the routine had changed, the whole bed, they must have built bigger lifts, went down to a pre-med room, adjacent to the operating theatre. My blood pressure and temperature were taken. I got my message across to the anaesthetist who seemed singularly unimpressed, he gave me a jab and within seconds I was no longer on this planet.

I came round back in my room. I had no idea what time it was but I felt quite comfortable, no pain, just drowsy. I saw a stand at the side of the bed on which hung two plastic bags of liquid. A tube attached the smaller one to my left wrist; the other vanished under the bedclothes, further down. I drifted off.

The next time I came round Mr Martinez was standing at the side of the bed. His look was confidently re-assuring as he told me everything had gone well and all was normal. He explained the drip into my arm was the standard post operation boost to my system and there was a tube inserted, through my 'willy' up into my bladder, to assist in the healing process of the internal wound caused by the operation. It would, he added, be there for a couple of days, but I could get up and walk about, as the stand was mobile. Thank God for that, I thought, bedpans are an experience one can really live without. He left; advising me he would be back next day.

I had been a bit nervous when I had first 'come to', not knowing what to expect, but now was the time to take stock. First, check 'willy'. It was still there — sigh of relief — and two plastic tubes were stuck up it. Sorry but they were, there is no other way of putting it. Strangely, and this may come as a surprise, there was no discomfort. The tube coming from the feeder bottle, high on the stand, had a glass phial and a tap with which you could control the flow into the body. The other tube ran to a draining bag at the foot of the trolley and was slowly filling with a blood coloured liquid. I was being gently flushed out.

The nurse came and removed the drip from my arm, adjusted my pillows, made me comfortable and I surveyed the scene. Carlos, who had been very quiet, allowing me to have my space so to speak, which I fully appreciated, thinking that maybe he was as an experienced hospital patient as I was. We conversed for a while but the reason for his hospitalisation still did not come up. It crossed my mind that he may be there for the same reason as I was, but still would not talk about it, even in these intimate circumstances. Being Latin he was probably more 'macho' than I was. Anyway he was happy and I got the impression he was nearer to departing than arriving. From the hospital, that is.

I surveyed my locker. The mandatory bowl of grapes had yet to materialise. There were two large bottles of water which, the nurse had told me I had to drink at least four a day. My two-day-old Sunday paper was still there, great, and underneath it were the two little bags of hard toast, left there from the meal tray of the previous night. Ah, I thought, not exactly mouth-watering 'canapés' but a little something before the meal I was expecting halfway through the night — well around 9.30pm.

The toast. Now I think I am much the same as anyone else when it comes to opening anything, that is wrapped in plastic — totally without a clue as to how to handle it. This wrapping is obviously a product of space age technology. It is so tough that I am sure that a packet of biscuits could be fired at the moon and reach there quite safely, certainly unopened, without the help of a spaceship. I once ordered, from a catalogue, one of those gadgets, a Bullworker I think it was called, that you exercise with and in a few days it builds you a body like Superman. Well, I couldn't even tear open the wrapping it came in. I didn't have the strength. So I sent it back. Let them 'Kick sand in my face' see if I care.

I picked up the bag of toast and pulled at the wrapper — nothing happened. I gripped it with my teeth and pulled at it with one hand — nothing happened. I took a firmer grip and pulled with both hands. Bang! The bag literally exploded like a firecracker. Sharp little crumbs went everywhere in the bed and although they changed my sheets, by request, at least twice, I swear I never did get rid of those crumbs. I was to curse them, even more, later in the day.

CHAPTER SIX

Visiting times were pretty free and easy in Spanish hospitals, or probably in all hospitals that are divided into small rooms. 'Love of my...' came late in the afternoon with a wonderful assortment of fruit — yes, grapes included — and other goodies. We had a little time for me to go over my day and to catch up with the toings and froings of the outside world, before the Carlos family began to arrive. I say 'began to arrive' because that's how it was. It was a procession, a bit I thought, like Noah's Ark, they kept coming in two by two, different sizes, different breeds, different ages. Sons, daughters, brothers, sisters, aunts, uncles... And all such nice people. As soon as they entered, they respectfully stopped, put on a straight face, gave us a polite hand to the mouth, shoulder-raising grin and then burst on top of Carlos as if he had just won the lottery.And the noise, everyone talking — no shouting — at once. You had to hear it to believe it. As with all the Latin races they gave the same amount of credence to the rule 'Only two at a bed at any one time' as they did to any form of 'queuing'.

Unable to stand it any longer 'Love of my...' slipped, no barged, out of the room and came back with a nurse to install some semblance of order. The nurse explained the 'two to a bed rule...' and that I was still under the effects of major surgery. They were all so terribly nice about it. Carlos added some words very rapidly and with apologetic noises, much hugging and kissing, for Carlos, that is, half of them left. The noise from the remaining six gradually rose to its previous decibel height. 'Love of...' left me a more up-to-date paper, told me to get some rest, the chance would be a fine thing, and said she would be back after lunch the following day.

It was about then that I began to feel a bit of pressure at the bottom of my stomach.

I skimmed through the paper, couldn't concentrate. The Carlos family gradually left. The pressure down below grew a little; discomfort crept in.

I called the nurse, she came, and on inspection we discovered between us that any pressure exerted on the lower stomach caused a rise in discomfort. She left and returned with the ward sister. After a brief survey and a rapid discussion the nurse left and returned with a replacement bag for the discharged fluid. The bag was fitted, the discomfort eased almost immediately, and with an exchange of smiles all round I was left to doze. As well as I could, that is, with my fellow bedmates, the crumbs of toast.

Because of the plumbing fittings I could only sleep on my back, or slightly to the left side as that was the way the pipes went. I am, by nature a right-sided sleeper, so I slept fitfully and cannot remember the exact passing of time that evening and the rest of the night. I came round at one time; the room was in semi-darkness. Carlos was watching the television and I had the discomfort of the pressure in my bladder. Carlos was actually asleep, which is the best way to spend your time in hospital. I called the nurse. No response. I called again; I felt I was being a nuisance. On the third call she arrived, peeling off the other rubber glove as she came in — I had obviously interrupted something. I hadn't seen this nurse before; the night shift had assumed control.

In a way I missed the big open ward where there was always something going on and you could see, sitting at a desk in the middle of the ward, a nurse readily available with a call, a wave of the arm, or in some cases, if necessary to catch attention in the early hours of the morning, the throwing of a pillow. But, in a small room ward you can get a sense of panic. Just pressing a button. Is it ringing, flashing somewhere out there? Can anyone hear?

I explained the source of my discomfort and pointed out that the bag at the bottom of the stand was full and needed changing. She left and returned with the night ward sister. Again they appraised the situation, had a brief rapid conversation, the nurse was dispatched and returned with fresh supplies and both bags were replaced. They left me and I settled down.

I was not in an over-relaxed frame of mind, which had cleared of any dizziness left behind by the operation. Something was bothering me. I decided to take a closer look at my newly installed plumbing arrangements. It struck me immediately. It was so obvious. The bag above, that held the fluid that was flushing me out was considerably bigger than the receiving bag at the end of the cycle. I was also, as instructed, drinking copious amounts of water, so the lower bag would obviously fill up and when it did the fluid had nowhere to go except back up into my bladder or anywhere else it could find. I had found the source of my discomfort and the solution was simple, put a bigger bag at the end of the cycle.

I settled back and was about to press the call button when I thought No. I had obviously interrupted something of importance a short while ago, I'l caring chap that I am, and wait patiently — well a patient — keep an eye on things and call only the bag needed replacing.

It was about then, that from somewhere close came the sound of a very loud moan. Not continuou but expelled as and when someone was breathing out, punctuated every few moments by an even louder wail.

In large open wards in hospitals, a comradeship develops between the patients. A bond of mutual understanding that everyone is equal and the focus, both for yourself and everyone else, is to get well and to get out. There is also a total acceptance of what is. The truth is never hidden or even belittled and this shows itself in a lot of the humour. For example, if we all know old Fred in the corner by the door is ninety-four and has pneumonia, we all know that his days are numbered. So you will hear comments like "Old Fred's gonna be lucky, he won't be here for Sunday lunch". A jibe aimed at hospital food, and not always justified, rather than at Fred. Or the doctor, who says to a patient just coming round from surgery, "I have some good news and some bad news. The good news is we cut off the right leg. The bad news is we gave away the wrong shoe."

A great deal of our humour is based on other people's misfortune and there is a cruelty, a callousness about it, that is a bit tongue-in cheek, but it can also be very real.

I recall a hospital ward I was in where an elderly gentleman, in about the same condition as old Fred, was moaning continuously. He was not aware he was doing it. The nurse changed his position many times, to no avail. The moaning continued. It went on and on. The ward was restless, you could feel it, no one was asleep, the moaning continued. Then a loud voice declared "For God's sake hurry up and die". You could feel the silence. A few seconds passed like a year. Then after another 'year' had passed another voice in a very House of Commons' accent, said slowly and deliberately "He-ah. He-ah." After another poignant moment there was a chorus of "Hear Hears" followed by laughter. The tension had been broken but for a moment the feeling that had been expressed in that callous cry had been unanimously agreed with by the whole 'house'.

Little was I to know that feeling was to return this night, though I did not have the comradeship of the other patients to back me up.

I lay awake. What with keeping an eye on the slowly filling waste bag and the moaning and wailing from down the corridor, sleep was out of the question. The decibel rating of the moaning varied bringing some relief. Carlos slept; perhaps he had got used to it. I prayed that I would.

The bag was nearly full. I called the nurse. Immediate response. Her smile almost preceded her into the room. I pointed to the bag, at which she looked and understood, she turned to go. I called her and explained as well as I could, in my halting Spanish, the difference in the size of the two bags. "That one up there is much bigger than that one down there. Bring a bigger bag". She, and the smile turned, went away and returned with what I could see was quite plainly the same size bag. I tried to get it across that it would make her life easier and mine a lot less fraught, if she got a bigger bag. To no avail. She rearranged my sheets, disturbed a few more crumbs of toast, and left the room, with a smile of course. The moaning continued. Carlos slept. I lay awake.

The moaning continued endlessly. 'For God hurry up and...' No. I must not think like that some unearthly reason that catchy little song from film 'A life of Brian' came into my head 'Always look the bright side of life'.

I smiled, what else could I do?

I caught the sister as she looked in. Again I explained the bag size difficulty, which she eventually understood but explained that it was a kit and that I would have to speak to my doctor about it in the morning. In the meantime she assured me, they would keep a close eye on the situation and check the level at frequent intervals. I should try and get some sleep.

Maybe I dozed, I know I certainly wished that fella' down the corridor would hurry up and... No no I didn't. I got through the night eventually without too much discomfort.

When I awoke, the daytime nursing staff had taken over. I realised this when a nurse I had never seen before came in to check us out and made a particular note of checking the lower disposal bag. Things are looking up, I thought.

Breakfast was served, temperatures taken, beds were straightened, all the usual activities of a ward coming to life. The moaning was notable by its absence. Maybe he 'hadn't made it through the night...' Shuu'sh.

Breakfast had unfortunately added to the 'hospital grits' as I had renamed them — the toast crumbs in the bed. Catching the eye of the 'nurse I had never seen before' she managed, by rolling me from one side to the other, to sweep most of them out of the bed. As events were to turn out I was to recall that rolling action quite vividly.

It was sometime in the late morning that I began to get 'that same old feeling that I get inside' of discomfort in the lower abdomen. I checked the disposal bag. No that was OK. In fact it was quite empty. Time passed, the discomfort increased.

I called the nurse, she came and went and returned with the sister. The in-going drip was working, there was plenty of room in the disposal bag. They had a murmured conversation and left.

Time passed. The discomfort increased to such an extent that I turned the drip-tap off and called the nurse. My action was, of course, looked upon as some kind of rebellion and it caused all sorts of furore. Soon my bed was surrounded I was sure, by everyone who was working on the ward. Mr Martinez, who, it now appeared obvious had been called earlier on, and for whom they had been waiting, followed them shortly afterwards. After a brief discussion wherein I enlightened him of my views on bag sizes and my discomfort, he waved to the nurse to pull back my covering sheet.

It was at this moment that the room, in my eyes, took over the appearance of a film studio, shooting a scene from one of those 'Carry on Doctor' movies. My bladder had enough and had decided to join me in my protest. The pressure had grown to such an extent that with perfect timing, as the nurse pulled back the sheet, so the tubes shot out of my 'willy', like a bullet from a gun, followed by an enormous jet of reddish fluid that quickly spread all over the bed. I yelped. The relief I felt was orgasmic.

CHAPTER SEVEN

It was at that very moment that I noticed a movement by the door. 'Love of my life' had come on an early visit. I can remember to this day, the look that came over her face. It was unforgettable. Well, imagine it. There was her dearly beloved, lying on a hospital bed, stark naked, yelling out, pissing blood in no uncertain manner and surrounded by a doctor and half a dozen nurses! The 'nurse whom I had never seen before', with great presence of mind, hurriedly took her by the arm, closed the door and evidently managed to explain that all was not as bad as it looked.

Meanwhile back at the bed, the scene had changed to resemble a pit stop in a Grand Prix, the nurses working in pairs, much like mechanics changing a wheel, stripped all the bedding, sheets, under sheets, rubber sheets, you name it. I wished I had had a stop-watch, or even better a frantic Murray Walker commentary. It was all done in seconds. My sense of relief was heightened by the thought that at last I may have got rid of those 'hospital-grits'.

Mr Martinez had quickly assessed the situation. He had sent for a tube with a slightly larger diameter, which momentarily boosted my ego — of course I needed a bigger tube, you only had to look down... Where... oh well... maybe not. Anyhow he inserted the tube up into my bladder, which, to my surprise, was quite painless. He then explained that the tube should be held in a straight line as far as possible and then curve gently into the disposal bag at the foot of the bed.

In order to effect this he took a small plastic bottle of cleaning fluid that was periodically inserted into the down tube to assist in the flushing process. He then took a length of one-inch bandage, attached one end to the neck of the bottle and the other end loosely but effectively to my 'willy'. He then dropped the bottle over the end of the bed! OUCH! No, I jest. It was a plastic bottle almost empty and it would, he explained, stop the tube from 'kinking' which was presumably the problem caused when I rolled over to get rid of those dammed 'bits of toast'.

He told me I could get up later in the day, but took no notice whatsoever of my theories on the problems created by the difference in size of the two bags. He smiled when I suggested that I would willingly buy a five-litre bottle of water, hastily drink the contents and install that at the end of the line. That was the only response I got — a smile. It was left as it was, but at least everyone was now aware that it had to be closely watched.

At the first sign that order had been restored in room 205, 'Love of my life' came through the door, quicker than a bargain hunter on the first day of a Harrods' sale. The early visit was occasioned, first of course to see how I had got through the night and secondly, to avoid as far as possible the altercations of the family and friends of Carlos. Who had, I must say, tolerated the fracas with more than stoic resistance. He had not spoken or moved during the whole performance, apart from the odd smile and the mandatory international thumbs up.

Before the local invasion arrived I managed to convince 'Love of my…' that I wasn't in pain; that I hadn't experienced any pain, and indeed on reflection, the scene she had witnessed was definitely out of 'Carry on Nurse'; although she could see no resemblance in me to Kenneth Williams and, no stretch of the imagination could turn any one of the Spanish nurses into Hattie Jacques.

The local police must have put a crowd limit on the number of visitors to Carlos as the afternoon slipped quietly by. 'Love of my…' left, not entirely convinced that there was an amusing side to the earlier performance, and I settled down, looking forward to an evening of football on the television. United were playing a team from mainland Spain in the European Cup. Prior to this I took a preliminary trial walk about with my mobile stand, out of the ward and along the sunlit balcony — very pleasant and again totally pain free so long as you remembered to keep the stand moving at the same pace as yourself.

Carlos, the 'Lucha' wrestling fan, had not yet retired to his bed so I asked him to put the television on and switch it to the right station for the football. He did so but only with a great show of reluctance. He then picked up his book and sat down, very upright in his chair, a posture I read to indicate disapproval. Sure enough, after considerable mutterings to himself, halfway through the first half he stood up, walked over to the TV set and turned it off! He then went back to his chair, completely ignoring me, picked up his book and sat down.

That ugly word 'gob-smacked' is the only word that adequately expressed my feelings. How could anybody do such a thing! My remonstrations — no, my rantings and ravings — eventually got him to turn it on again and repair to the nearby public lounge until the game was over. But this was only after he had taken some time to enlighten me with his opinion, which boiled down to his belief, that you can only be considered a sportsman if you played for the love of the game and not for money, and that modern-day footballers had gone too far down the one road to be worthy of any consideration whatsoever. In truth I had used many of the points that he raised in many pub discussions that I had been involved in. So my mood mellowed, I returned to the TV. Only to find that I had missed what turned out to be the only two goals of the match. I began to believe that you truly could not win 'em all...

The few days that I had to spend in hospital passed pleasantly enough. I read a lot, did not watch much television, only the 'Lucha' wrestling — yes, there is quite a lot of it on Canarian TV. I had by now forgiven Carlos and he almost had me totally converted.

I walked the outside terraces pushing my mobile plumbing apparatus, the sun glinting off the plastic bags. The lower bag held the clue as to how well you were progressing. For the first day or so, the fluid would be a rich 'burgundy', as the days passed it faded to a 'rose' but only when it reached and maintained a 'sauterne' was there any chance of you being allowed out.

The colour of your bag therefore became the first topic of conversation when you met a fellow patient who had undergone the same operation or something similar. On one of my first circuits of the balcony I bumped... No, I didn't actually bump, that could have been painful, if not fatal — rather I met the wife of a friend, who unbeknown to me, and indeed, I think to any other of their friends, had just had an hysterectomy — perhaps that is another subject that is not talked about. Anyway she was equipped with what looked like the same additional plumbing that I had. Each time we met we checked the colour of each other's bags and exchanged such comments as "You won't be going home yet, then" or "Looks good, you could be out tomorrow".

In some ways it felt as if we were having an intimate relationship. Well, what would you call exchanging opinions on the colour of each other's 'pee' with your friend's wife, whilst dressed in your pyjamas!

After three or four days had passed I reached and maintained very acceptable 'chablis' colour and Mr Martinez allowed me to go home.

CHAPTER EIGHT

It was one week to the day that I returned to the hospital for a progress appointment.

A Spanish hospital waiting room is the absolute archetypal example that the word queue is not in their language. A free-for-all is acted out with a sort of refined, determined somnolence. The best advice is to arrive early, determine the door of your particular consultant's office and lean on that door — well, on the doorjamb. If you have been beaten to this pole position, patrol the nearby vicinity, in the said casual, determined, somnolent manner, but being acutely aware of any movement by the door so you can jump, yes, literally jump, into the pole position. This is the only sure way of avoiding a possible two or three hour wait. Of course, if you are on crutches, or carrying a limb, this may not be possible. In which case take along a well-briefed, athletic colleague.

This technique may not gain you immediate entry because another patient, with a bit more clout than you have, that is a relative of the mayor, a senior policeman's wife, a friend of a friend of the doctor, the local newspaper delivery boy, that sort of person, may be called, by name to come forward. But at least you're in the pole doorjamb position. From where, when the door opens you have a chance of catching the consultant's eye, he then knows you are there, he is expecting to see you, so the next time someone comes out you go in, with a set smile on your face and air of confident authority.

Mission accomplished. We sat in front of Mr Martinez.

He sat there, elbows on the arm-rests, end of fingers tapping together, you know the scene, allowing me to tell him what had been happening to me during the last week and he repeatedly nodded inferring that everything was looking normal. As indeed it was. I had no side-effects. I was not over-frequently 'peeing', I had a good strong jet, and no dribbling and my sexual appetite seemed positively blooming. In fact I was on top of the world. I could not have felt more pleased with the way things had gone.

His secretary, who had been taking notes, was checking the diary for the next appointment date when Mr Martinez opened the file she had previously handed to him.

At this point you may be thinking that he should have referred to the notes before he saw me. Well, of course he should have. But you must appreciate that we had more or less forced our way in, giving him no time to appraise himself with my case.

"Ah, Ah!" he murmured, and after reading for a short while he added, "We do have a problem."

I, by nature, was reading the notes upside-down — many people who have been in sales most of their lives develop this somewhat nefarious talent — and I had already seen, in capital letters, the word CARCINOMA which I knew to be the Latin and the Spanish for CANCER.

The laboratory report on the analysis of the parts of the prostate gland that they had cut away stated 'young, newly formed cancer cells to be present'. There. I had it — THE BIG C.

47

I can only liken the shock of that moment, even now, after having had all of eight years to recall it, as at one moment, I was running through the countryside, feeling the wind and summer sun on my face, the smell of new mown hay, a blue sky and nothing but a beautiful view in front of me and suddenly from out of nowhere I hit a very solid glass wall.

The shock was immense. After all I had gone through, feeling so lucky to have had no pain, no side-effects — to get hit with this.

I cannot say I remember exactly the rest of what was said at that appointment. I vaguely recall bits and pieces — alternative forms of treatment, further tests which would have to be arranged and would I call his office...

We rose, and left in a dazed silence. As if in a nightmare we floated over that vast floor of the reception area, then suddenly I felt my feet came back to earth with a spine-jolting thump. I refused to accept that I had cancer cells in my body. Physically I was going to act sensibly and follow the hospital's guidance but mentally I couldn't acknowledge the cells were there. I could not feel them. I did not have them when I walked into the hospital less than two hours ago, and there was no way I was going to walk out with them.

Strange as it may seem, I felt very strong at that moment. I was through the wall.

Cancer is not an easy topic to discuss at any time, let alone under these circumstances, even with someone who is very close. We hugged a lot, we cried as little as we could and we came to the decision that whatever further tests and treatments I had to have, I would have them back in the UK.

This decision was not based on any wavering of confidence in the Spanish health system, whatever you may surmise from my meanderings, but simply because I would feel better and have more confidence being treated in my own language. Most doctors including the Spanish would agree with that.

Mr Martinez understood completely and arranged for me to have all the test results, slides and X-rays. He could not have been more helpful.

'Young and newly formed', they were the words that spurred me to action. Most of us are aware I believe, that the majority of cancers can be cured if they are caught very early. If I had them in my body — and I was still not convinced, despite the medical evidence that I had — then they were not going to be there for long.

Within a week I had returned to London, had seen my GP, who obtained for me an appointment with The Middlesex Hospital in Mortimer Street.

I was living in a flat just off Marylebone Road, nearer to Edgeware Road underground station than Baker Street, but within a comfortable walk to the hospital.

It was the summer of '93 and the sun shone warmly on the streets of London. Streets that were in an area that it was a pleasure to walk through, lined with Regency terraces and divided by rustic-mews. Streets with historically nostalgic names: Wimpole, Harley, Baker, Oxford, Regent and not so far away the freshness of Regents Park. To the south the wonders of Selfridges and to the east all those fascinating 'emporia' that line Tottenham Court Road and sell all things electrical from a humble toaster to the latest product from the imaginative mind of Mr Bill Gates and his like. Central London is a wonderful place to live in summer, especially if you don't have to commute.

I was quite well acquainted with The Middlesex, having had to spend a couple of months there way back in 1951 when, as an up-and-coming Denis Compton, I tried to catch a cricket ball with my nose playing cricket for my school against Kingsbury County in the suburbs of northwest London.

When the accident happened, my headmaster, who lived in nearby Harrow and was watching the game, put me in his car and drove me to the nearest hospital. They advised us that they did not operate an emergency service on a Saturday morning! Not too much of the caring 'Cottage' about that.

Unbelievably we got the same response from several other hospitals and that is how a young lad with a seriously bent 'hooter' and two black eyes, who lived in Hendon on the outskirts of London, found himself in a hospital in the middle of the West End. The reason I was in there for so long was that after they had straightened it out, it began to bleed and bleed and bleed. It took a long time before they could to get it to stop. I believe I got a mention in the Medical Press for having, up to that time, the largest quantity of blood by transfusion for a minor injury. But that's another story.

1951 was the year of The Great Exhibition, when the Royal Festival and Queen Elizabeth Halls were built on the south bank of the Thames. All I saw of that exhibition was the tip of the Skylon from the window of the plastic surgery ward on the top floor of the hospital. The Skylon, a tall grey-coloured, cigar-shaped object pointing to the heavens, had no political, social or religious significance that I could fathom as I lay gazing at it day in, day out, holding a bowl under my nose to catch the blood. They later moved me to the Ear, Nose and Throat ward, which had much better scenery —

no badly burnt bodies and faces. And so my hospital experience started to accumulate.

Nursing is of course, a vocation in the fullest divine meaning of the word. That is as true today as it was then, except that in the fifties, to be a nurse at The Middlesex you had to be either a debutante with at least a double-barrelled surname, or the daughter of an Irish nobleman. At least that is what it seemed like then. Anyway, they were all absolute angels — and still are — and I was very pleased to be back in the care of 'The Old Lady of Mortimer Street', The Middlesex.

CHAPTER NINE

After all that I had been through at no time had I felt any pain. OK a little discomfort when I was struggling to 'pee' — the occasional acute embarrassment that that caused was more painful — there was nothing to make me aware that something was wrong. In fact I felt fitter than I had for a long time. The one side-effect from the prostatectomy was retarded ejaculation, and although I must admit to a slightly diminished sensitivity at the actual crucial moment, I could live with that. The 'young newly formed cancer cells' that were found in the biopsy, they were another story.

So there I was, feeling fit and heavily bronzed from the Canarian sun, yearning to be on the first tee at Wentworth — or any golf club, come to that — walking the beautiful sunlit streets of London towards the UCH Nuclear Institute of Medicine. 'Nuclear' — as in physics? Weapons? Hiroshima — or to do with 'my privates'? It was unbelievable and it must be happening to some one else.

Taking into consideration my age and the state at which the cancer was at, it was recommended that I undergo a course of external radiotherapy. I accepted the recommendation. I was advised of the possible side-effects which were basically the same as those of the first operation, i.e. possible incontinence, retrograde ejaculation (got that), impotency, etc, but also, during the course of the treatment I might feel nauseous, bleeding whilst going to the toilet — both ways — suffer pain whilst going to the 'loo', feel tired and listless but I would recover from these in due course, that is, if I were to get them in the first place. Whoow! 'Here's looking at you kid'.

I was put into the caring hands of The Department of Oncology and more specifically into the equally caring hands of a charming lady, Dr Duncan. She made arrangements for me to have the necessary body-scan and Ulta-sound scan. The latter being one of those comparatively recent inventions that can detect lumps and bumps inside your body, one up on the X-ray that basically sees bones. It is the technique that is used to look at babies through the wall of the tummy. With a prostate scan they ask you to... yes, you got it... drop your trousers and pants, lie on the couch and face the wall. Then a probe from outer space... No, no, no from the scanner, is inserted into your rectum and pictures of your prostate are obtained.

During one of these scans, I cannot recall which one, three indigo marks were made on my body, one on the outside of each hip and one dead centrally just above my 'willy'. I surmised that these would be the target spots for the radiation beams to be aimed at during the treatment. It crossed my mind that I hoped the operator was a reasonably good dart player and that double top was his/her favourite finish.

Dr Duncan explained that the treatment would be given over a period of three consecutive weeks and that I should attend the radiotherapy unit, based under the Oncology Out Patients at 11.15am on Monday through Friday. Fifteen sessions in all.

On the first Monday morning I stepped out into the bright sun feeling a little apprehensive, but a brisk pace soon took me down Crawford Street, across Baker Street over Portland Place and Great Portland Street into Cleveland Street and under the shadow of the Post Office Tower — Ooops. I had gone a bit too far — round into Nassau Street and down into the unknown, the basement below the Oncology Department. What should I expect? I didn't even know what Oncology meant!

I was early but that didn't interfere with the welcoming smile from the receptionist, who asked me to take a seat, I would only have to wait a short while.

Within minutes I was collected and led down a gentle ramp into the bowels of the building. We entered a room which contained a large machine in the shape of a circle with a couch, or trolley that could obviously slide through the middle of the hoop. One of the operators asked me to slip my trousers down and lie on the trolley. I did and naturally, turned to face the wall. No, I must lie on my back fold my arms across my chest and keep perfectly still.

The machine moved menacingly over me. It stopped pretty well immediately over my 'willy'. Ah, they were lining up on the indigo marks. (Any of you girls play darts?) They told me to hold my position, it would only take a few minutes, and then they presumably left the room. I was on my own, no, not entirely, me and a piece of nuclear plant. He buzzed. I said nothing. The girls returned, the machine backed off, I was back on my feet, dress adjusted and back up the ramp with a cheerful 'See you tomorrow' ringing in my ears. That was it. Was that all there was to it?

I took a left turn out of the hospital and with a light heart and a bounce in my step turned south into Tottenham Court Road, left into New Oxford Street, left again and down the steps into Waggamama's. I was in the mood to do something and this little Japanese — sort of fast food, canteen style noodle restaurant — was just the place. I had a bowl of spicy prawn noodles, with a side plate of chicken wings and a large Sapporo beer. And I thought to myself, I can handle this — not the noodles far too difficult, where's the fork? — the Nuclear medicine... no problem. Yes I will have another beer. (Who mentioned the waistline?) Cheers.

All in all, considering the treatment I was undergoing the three weeks passed quickly and pleasantly. I did not eat so exotically every day, but by taking a different route every time I got to know the area pretty well.

The possibility of suffering from any of the side-effects never entered my head. I never experienced one of them. In fact, it must have been half way through the course of my daily 'Chernobyl showers' that I asked Dr Duncan if the machine, 'Buzz 22', I think it was called, was actually working, as up until now I hadn't felt a thing.

"It happens to some of the fortunate ones," she smiled. I half smiled back. The really fortunate ones would not be here, but I knew what she meant.

At the end of the treatment I was relatively 'scar-free', physically and mentally; my PSA reading was down to 0.7 and in order to keep an eye on me I was put on a three-monthly check-up schedule.

CHAPTER TEN

I had work to do so I returned to the Canaries. In truth, as much as I loved London in the summer, I was missing the champagne air, the beautiful clear blue sky and the unpolluted beaches that I had grown used to over the last nine years of living in those islands. I felt fresh and re-invigorated. I knew inside me that I could beat this malignancy and the absence of any side-effects only strengthened that belief.

Absence of any side-effects? My sex life was not what it should be. OK, as I have said I had accepted and learnt to live with retrograde ejaculation but this was something else! I could get sexually aroused, get a sort of erection, but I could not keep it up. Any attempt at getting on with the job was out of the question and totally out of hand.

I recalled once being in the company of a very elderly man, and as we both watched a gorgeous mini-skirt sway by, he commented, with an understanding that only comes with the status of being 'elderly', "They can take away the ability but they can't take away the inclination." I could see now exactly what he meant, exactly what he was feeling, but 'Heaven help us' I wasn't anywhere near that stage of my life.

At first I told myself, no, I wished, I prayed that it was just a temporary effect of the radiotherapy, that it

would eventually wear off and everything would be normal,
 'There IS nothing wrong with my willy'. There CAN'T be. I won't allow it. Me, a tall relatively attractive (so I have been told on the odd... no, numerous occasion) 'man about town sort of fella' and can't get it up! It is just not possible. 'IT CAN'T HAPPEN TO ME' I inwardly screamed. But it did.
 Impotent. There it is, that is the word. I'll say it again — IMPOTENT. Right from the very moment you start to tell yourself 'There is nothing wrong with my willy', that is the word you will not take in. You refuse even to recognise it. For God's sake I can't even pronounce it correctly. When I think of it — I always back off actually saying it — it always sounds like 'impudence'. I wished in the name of 'Thesaurus' that was just what it was, a bold impertinent presumption.
 But it wasn't. It was there in all its confidence-sapping reality. Throughout the whole of my treatment, right from the very first I had always counted my blessings, always thinking positive, always believing that everything would be all right in the end. And now this. Impotent. So help me I would have willingly suffered every other side-effect, temporary or permanent, than end up with this one. Let me suffer some pain, let me have difficulty passing water, let me dribble a bit — I'll wear the bloody nappy, I'll take the interrupted painful bowel movements. Anything but this!
 At the end of the day, deep down within himself a man knows that he is the hunter, the predator, the warrior, the stalker, (nice word that, appropriate, if you can forget the present day inferences). His masculinity, which can be expressed in many ways, is all-important. All right, I am aware that we live in a world

of equal rights and I am not against that — well, not entirely — and I recall a piece of 'graffiti' from the '60s, that proclaimed 'Support Women's Lib, make him sleep on the wet patch'. If only. Also a man can fail in many ways and still survive in his community. He can fail to get promotion. He can fail to be a good husband, a good father or even a good friend. He can fail in all these things and get away with it because his 'macho-ism' won't allow him to see it. He's failed in someone else's eyes; he can hide it from himself.

But, when 'You can't get it up' then you know, you really know you have failed. You can't kid yourself; there is nowhere to hide. In the animal kingdom you would probably distance yourself from the herd, live a solitary life on a far-away plain. Impotence comes with a primeval, instinctive feeling of no longer belonging, of having no right to be there. But we are human — life goes on. 'Say yes to it, and go forward.'

'Love of my life' was absolutely marvellous, as she had been right from the start. She lightened the whole thing. Tremendous support, love, affection and most of all fun. She never allowed either of us to feel low. I cannot emphasise enough how important it is to have the complete understanding of the feelings of each other, and for each other, at all times.

Without 'Love of my' I could well have curled up into a little ball and given up. With her and with my in-born Sagittarian optimism we went forward. We had a problem, but a problem is only the start of a solution. Recalling some of the things that we had read or heard about, we knew, though knowing nothing specific, that there was an answer, and that we would find it.

I soon got back into the 'manana' way of life, so rightly favoured by the Canarians, allowing myself plenty of time to take in the sun, swim and enjoy the local fish, on a plate that is, and the occasional bottle of wine. Looking back I can't see why I didn't go back to London and demand some action to put it right. I suppose the ever hopeful, but slowly dying thought, that it was only a temporary aberration, held me back. Was I still kidding myself? The 'taboo' subject, don't talk about it. I certainly could not discuss such a subject on the phone. So I waited. Things did not improve.

The weeks running up to that first check-up crawled by, not with any physical pain or discomfort but, mentally, I had put myself in a sort of 'limbo', a protective suspension, trying to believe that this could not be happening to me, but being continually reminded at all the wrong moments that it could, and it was. Perhaps I should have returned earlier than I did. If I had the time over again I would have.

My body or more specifically my 'plumbing apparatus' had, with the one enormous exception, returned to complete normality. I was 'peeing' regularly, litres of it with a good strong flow, so I was emptying my bladder — very important that, emptying your bladder. By the way they have a machine that can measure your flow-rate and volume, a sort of 'pee-ometer', what an amazing world we live in. Everything in the 'willy' department was fine. I just wished he would stand up for himself every now and again.

I returned to London several days before my appointment to give a blood sample, so that my PSA reading would be available. The blood samples were taken in an annexe to the hospital in Cleveland Street which, way back in the fifties had housed the Athletes Clinic. A place, where, under the NHS, you could take your sports injury, sit in a queue in the waiting room, without an appointment and get absolutely top rate treatment. They certainly kept me in a tracksuit for more years than I had expected. It was also quite surprising whom you saw there. I remember being in front of an athlete I recognised, Don Thompson, who was to go on and win the Gold Medal in the 50-kilometre walk in the 1960 Rome Olympics. He was the current European champion.

I insisted he went in front of me — it seemed the least I could do for my country. Can you imagine any of today's athletes queuing for treatment in a National Health hospital!

Every time, when I enter a blood clinic, I recall the Tony Hancock TV episode called 'The Blood Donor'. It lightens the occasion, for I am sure that none of us —almost none of us — like needles being pushed into us, albeit to pump something in or to pull something out. The staff here, in their calm professional manner, take considerably less than the 'immortalised' armful and it's all over in a matter of seconds.

I saw Dr Duncan at her usual Wednesday morning clinic. Sometimes, not always, student doctors accompany her. They were there on this occasion and both of them were female. Well they would be, wouldn't they, on this occasion!

My PSA reading had not shifted, which was fine. I addressed the group and told them that, to all intents and purposes, the lower half of my body was working absolutely fine, with one gigantic exception — and how in the name of The Karma Sutra was I going to tell three attractive females about that?

"I can't get it... I can't get a proper erection," I said as boldly as I could without averting my eyes. Dr Duncan looked up; she had probably experienced moments like this before, which prompted that look of painful understanding that showed, momentarily, in her eyes.

She took control of the situation immediately. The two students sat very still, so did I. I was over the first hurdle; I was out in the open now. I explained in more detail the problems I was experiencing and Dr Duncan, with regard to the students as well as myself went through the whys and wherefores of impotency occurring. Of course I had been aware of it as a possible side-effect. In the back of my mind I had known it was a possibility way back when I stood, covered in embarrassment, in that crowded bar and made the decision to have the operation, but I never thought it would actually happen to me. I had been under the scalpel and had come out unscathed so I had been full of confidence and optimism. 'There is nothing wrong with my willy'. 'Buzz 22' had other ideas — he played a different game.

Dr Duncan added that impotency was a specialist subject; she would give me an introduction to a consultant in that field, Mr Abbot, and that I should phone his secretary for an appointment. In the meantime, keeping an ever-watchful eye, I was to return to see her in three months' time.

I felt a little more comfortable within myself, at last something was happening. The last few months had been more than a little harrowing. 'Love of my life' had come up with that marvellous little phrase 'Say yes to life and move on'. We managed.

I had also heard or read somewhere another aphorism 'There is no such thing as failure, there are only results'. I liked that one as well. I had good results that the cancer was in remission. It had not spread and my plumbing was working correctly. That must be a positive result. With regard to the other business — it was only the beginning, there was a lot more playing to go, goals to be scored. A result yet to be achieved.

CHAPTER ELEVEN

I arrived at Mr Abbot's consulting rooms a few days later at 10am. They were located in the same buildings as the Blood Clinic, and the old Athletes Clinic. I went up the stairs and sat in the already crowded waiting room. I had feelings I found difficult to describe. I looked around. Were all these men here for the same reason as I? Had they come to see a different doctor? Did the reception staff know why I was here? Well they knew whom I had come to see, so they must know. I tried to look nonchalantly at ease, totally relaxed. Why did I try to look like that? I had nothing to be ashamed of. Yes I had. I couldn't get it up! It was that old 'macho' thing again. Internally I cowered.

My name was called. I stood up. I felt like everyone was looking at me. They must know. 'Ah, who gives a shit'? (I must stop saying that) I followed the nurse with my head held high and a silly grin on my face, which didn't fool anyone — least of all myself. In fact I felt revolted that I had put it there. Here I was in the prime of life, 6ft 4in tall, in better shape than a lot of men that I knew who were twenty years younger and I couldn't get it...!

I was praying the man I was about to see could perform miracles.

Mr Abbot was a middle-aged man, steel grey hair, dressed in a grey suit with waistcoat, with an easy smile and a firm handshake. On his righthand side sat an attractive Indian lady, complete with sari, covered with an open white coat. For some reason, which I could not fathom, considering the reason I was there, her presence did not bother me. Perhaps it was because she reminded me of Madhur Jaffrey, the well-known Indian actress and celebrated TV chef — I have all her recipe books. Oh, that I was just here for a cookery lesson.

Mr Abbot introduced her in a brief manner that told me she was there for the whole of the appointed time. An air of calm assurance was generated by the nod and half smile that she gave me. I accepted it and relaxed as well as I could — 'Say yes to life and go forward'. So there were Indians who had the same problem as I had. That had never crossed my mind; I thought I was the only one. You mean that this could be a worldwide problem; there could be millions out there like me. I wonder if they ever talk about it.

I explained my predicament to them both and with a little prompting from Mr Abbot I found I was able to explain and discuss the intimate details of my sex life quite readily.

Mr Abbot then took some time to explain that the failure to obtain or maintain an erection — he seemed to avoid the word impotence — can be created by psychological problems or as a direct result of an accident, or as in my case, suffered because of the treatment I had received.

A simple way to determine the difference between the causes, is that if you wake up in the morning with a very solid erection (I remember it well) which you obviously manifested whilst you were asleep, which dies on you and you are unable to regain it — try sleepwalking round to her side of the bed... No, no, I jest.

Oh. I don't know'... That may not be a bad... Anyway that almost certainly means that your problem is in your mind. Put there and nurtured by the stress, self-created by the worry and fear of impotency itself. You have got a chance; you can be taken in hand so to speak, and probably talked out of it.

On the other hand if you awaken with a very flaccid 'member' (what a funny name to call your 'willy'. What does it mean? That you belong to a club. If it does I certainly felt as if I had been 'black-balled') — then your problem is almost certainly physical, created, as in my case, by the radio-therapy treatment damaging the nerve ends that trigger the demand for the rush of blood to the spongy parts of the 'willy' that creates an erection. I unfortunately belonged, very firmly, no very 'flaccidly', to the second category.

Having had it determined for me, and having 'accepted' that I was never again going to be able to create my own erection, and, as I had not yet reached the time in my life when I wanted to give it up, I had to accept that I needed assistance. What assistance was there available and how acceptable was it? My logical brain, most Sagittarians are logical, told me that Mr Abbot was about to enlighten me.

Drastic needs, and I can assure you there is nothing more drastic to the male species, than not be able to... require drastic measures. Some of the measures I was to hear about were, to say the least, in my view, drastic.

They included a permanent surgical insertion, into the 'willy,' of a semi-rigid piece of plastic that you bent down for normal use and up for intercourse. This was obviously the root of all those 'or are you just glad to see me' jokes.

Another, again, required the insertion of flexible balloon type plastic pipes in the 'willy', a reservoir of fluid in the lower abdomen all connected to a hand-pump secreted in the scrotum — I leave you to work out the rest — but it brings a whole new meaning to the phrase 'I had him by the balls'.

Don't get me wrong, I am not denigrating these products, as I am sure they are used and very successfully at that — whatever turns you on — I merely aim to keep a sense of proportion and maintain a sense of humour, of fun, of light-heartedness about the whole thing. Believe me if you don't you are in for a very unhappy time.

Another method was by injection. Evidently there is a drug, closely related to morphine, which is obtained from the oriental poppy, which, when injected into the soft tissue of the 'willy' cause a swift increase to the blood supply, leading to an erection that could last up to two hours! Now there's a bit of 'one-up-manship' if ever there was — two hours, several 'up-mans-sh.'. If you see what I mean. Your 'willy' actually gets 'stoned'! It all sounds a bit too clinical for me and in any case you're bound to feel a bit of 'pri**'. No. No. I can't say that.

I could tell by the change in the tone of his voice that Mr Abbot favoured the vacuum method. This consists of a hand pump, a plastic cylinder, an assortment of rubber rings and a lubricant. The open end of the cylinder is lubricated and the rubber ring or a combination of rubber rings is stretched around the end. A plastic tube attaches the hand pump to the other end. You then place your 'willy' inside the cylinder and holding it firmly against your body, to ensure it is airtight, you utilise the hand pump. As the air is withdrawn from the cylinder so the blood rushes into your 'willy'. Hey presto you have an erection. You slip of the rubber rings at the base, which maintains your erection and you are ready for action for thirty minutes. The handbook advises thirty minutes as the maximum time you should keep the rings on and do not fall asleep with them on, otherwise you may damage blood vessels. Now this looked more acceptable, thirty minutes, eh. This could be a positive result. OK there are some pluses and some minuses.

Let's look at the pluses first. With experience you can control the consistency and rigidity of the erection and I'll let your fertile imagination make what you like out of that. I am also convinced that regular use of this method increases the size of your 'willy', albeit some medical minds may not concur.

The infamous 'Brewer's Droop' is banished forever. Once you and your loved one, have set the romantic scene, once your emotions, your mental feelings have subtly instructed your body what to do then, in the words of Ed Harris as only he could say them, in the film Appollo 13, ring out loud and clear, "Failure is not an option".

The big minus, and perhaps the only one, is the interruption to the flow of the occasion, going through all that rigmarole. It breaks up the spontaneity, which is sometimes vital to the magic of the moment. Well, some prior preparation in some circumstances can speed things up a bit, but it is something you have to work your own way around.

If you are a couple who can only get it off in weird and wonderful places, like 37000ft above the Atlantic or in the last empty carriage on the Northern Line underground between Hampstead Heath and Golders Green — the ultimate 'quickie' — or in Sainsbury's multi-storey car park late on a Friday evening — Yes you were seen — then you might have to change your mating habits. But that could also be a lot of fun — perhaps we should all do it anyway.

So overall the vacuum method seemed to be the most acceptable. All the parts came in a very nicely packed zippered case and included a comprehensive instruction book and, would you believe, a very detailed video! And in the words of the late Kenny Everett's outrageous character 'Cupid Stunt', 'It's all done in the best possible taste'.

Mr Abbot offered, there and then, to give me a trial run on the injection method. More out of curiosity rather than any serious conviction that I would ever use it, I accepted. They led me into an adjoining room. I removed my trousers and pants, and lay on the trolley and turned to face the w... No. No... covered by a sheet I propped myself up on my elbows. The Indian lady prepared a syringe. Mr Abbot pulled back the cover, picked up my 'willy' and indicated the fleshy parts where the needle should be inserted, no more than twelve times a month and always in a different place — on the 'willy' that is, not a different place like the Northern Line or Sainsbury's car park.

Prior to the highlight of a romantic evening this was the last thing I could envisage myself doing. But... you can get used to anything given the time and the motivation, just think of diabetics who have to use the needle regularly, it becomes a part of everyday life, just like making love.

The needle went in. I lay back. Mr Abbot said, "Right, we will leave you for little while. Try and get in the mood. You know what I mean."

To try and feel a little 'horny' under these conditions was, to say the least, a trifle optimistic. However after a little while 'willy' started to move. After a couple of minutes he was looking 100 per cent better than I had managed for some time.

They returned, "Well," asked Mr Abbot, in a very matter-of-fact sort of way, "how are we getting on?" The 'we' presumably was referring to 'willy' and me.

"Quite encouraging," I said, "better than anything I have experienced lately."

Mr Abbot lifted 'willy' squeezed him and let him drop. "Mmmm. I would not be very pleased with that." 'Madhur' did not look too impressed either.

"That should subside in a couple of hours. If it doesn't, come back to the clinic. You can get dressed now."

I tucked 'willy' back into my Y-fronts as best I could and followed them back into the outer office.

I could tell by the way that he never mentioned it again that Mr Abbot was as about as impressed with the injection method for me, as I was. After a brief discussion we both agreed it would be the vacuum cylinder, which I was surprised to find was not available from the NHS. A medical representative of the company that distributed the product was available at the hospital at certain times and I arranged to see him.

I shook them both by the hand, said my goodbyes and it was only later that I realised how marvellous, how professional they had been.

I walked as insignificantly as I could past the reception desk and across the still-crowded waiting room, very conscious of this unusual thing in my trousers. It seemed a shame to waste it, but then, as the doctor and 'Madhur' had said, it was not that impressive and it was already going 'cold-turkey'. I had a sudden fit of the 'munches' and so I stepped briskly out into the sunshine and headed straight for Waggamama's.

My appointment with the medical representative went very well, considering the sensitivity of both the subject and the product. We met as complete strangers but as we were in a hospital environment and both of us, having the same intention that neither of us was going to be embarrassed, we got on fine. He went through all the items in the well-organised zipper-pack they came in, and I followed with the manual. He asked me if I would like some time on my own to have a practice run, I asked if it was compulsory, he said no. I declined the offer stating that, with a very detailed instruction book and an explicit video, I was confident I could handle it. I paid a not inconsiderable amount of money and with a little black bag tucked under my arm, I stepped out into a new life.

Into a — new — life. I say it slowly and deliberately because looking back I found it very difficult to capture and express exactly how I felt through all the drama, and believe me, it was drama. Unless you have actually become impotent there is no way you can get near it. I know I couldn't, until it happened.

To get the point across in a cruder sort of way, we all sit on the toilet every day, every one of us — shit happens — there is nothing any one of us can do about it. OK, you can make it more acceptable, buy softer toilet tissue, put a garden in the closet, and install a bidet, it still happens. I didn't want to be impotent but I was. I didn't want to have to do something about it, ut I had to. I needed to. It happened, it was happening — there was nothing I could do about it.

'Say yes to a new life and move on' — that's what that little black bag, I held so tightly under my arm, meant to me.

Would I want anyone to know that I was impotent? Would I want anyone to know I had a prostate problem? 'There is nothing wrong with my "willy" and don't let anyone think that there is'. That used to be the way, now I am not so sure. It is not something I would bring up in everyday conversation, obviously, but in private if it were to help someone, of course.

Pub-talk, uttered by both sexes, like playground talk can be very cruel and if only those men who sneer and pass comments, such as 'Of course he didn't make it. He can't get it up, can he!' — would only realise, that there, but for the 'Grace of God', at that particular moment, go they. They have a one in three chance of getting a prostate problem and then a one in three chance of 'not being able to get it up'.

We all accept that what people do in the privacy of their own bedrooms is entirely their own business —some people take costumes, some resort to leather goods... it takes all sorts. We take a little black bag, it's as simple as that and we have had a smile on our face ever since.

CHAPTER TWELVE

I have made a point out of the fact that 'S**t' happens, there is nothing you can do about it, and I have likened that to the likelihood of the average male getting a prostate problem. Well, that is not exactly true. You can do something. It is all to do with not knowing that you are heading towards a problem. If you are totally unaware that you are running into danger, then you can't do anything about it. With the very likelihood of prostate problems in his latter years, what man is aware that he can, indeed, should do something about it in his earlier years? We don't talk about it — we are therefore not aware that it even exists What's more, because of its totally unacceptable social stigma, we don't want to know about it.

For every hour of every day of your life, your body is fighting, struggling to be healthy. I say fighting, struggling, to emphasis the point. There are many among us who endeavour to assist their bodies in this struggle on a daily basis; they exercise, they eat the right foods, they practise self control. Whereas the majority of us are heavily into self-abuse in one way or another — too much TV watching, too much alcohol, too much nicotine and an entirely unthinking, self-indulgence into anything we like the taste of. We have a totally uncaring, self-destructive attitude towards that one precious commodity we all own — our bodies.

'We are what we eat'. An old boring but true cliché. All the essential multi-vitamins, fatty acids, minerals and the other necessary items that our bodies need to be healthy can only come from what we put in our mouths.

It is no accident that in the East the incidence of prostate-related problems is considerably less than that encountered in the West. They also have fewer heart and cholesterol-based diseases than we have in the West. It is no coincidence that their diet is based more on fibre, grains, vegetables and fish, rather than the meat and dairy produce that we over-indulge in. When did you last see a herd of cattle or a flock of sheep in a photograph, or a picture, with a Chinese setting? Fields of rice and the odd chicken — yes. When have you ever seen a selection of oriental cheeses in a supermarket? Chinese Cheddar and Indonesian Edam and the like do not exist.

During the colonisation of the African continent and the subsequent introduction of the Western diet, the prostate problem increased markedly in the African man. This is related today in the fact that the Afro-American has a much higher incidence of prostate related-problems than does the American white-man. They can certainly run faster but whatever they take in as fuel promotes prostate problems, which they can't run away from. It may even suggest, and it is a theory supported by many, that such problems could be hereditary. So ask around the family — that is if you can get anyone to talk about it.

If we are what we eat and I've ended up with prostate cancer maybe something can be gained at looking back at my eating habits.

I was born in the mid-thirties of Scottish parents, therefore my mother was a good cook — all Scots women are good cooks. My early childhood took me through the Second World War, rationing books, which suggested we didn't over-indulge, fortified with powdered egg, orange juice and spoonfuls of Cod Liver Oil and Malt; my father had an allotment, so we had seasonable fresh 'veggies'. Sounds quite good so far. My mother, rightly or wrongly, allowed us a pint of milk every day and we got a third of a pint in the school morning break. Why is it that out of all the species in the animal kingdom, the human being is the only one that continues drinking milk after it has left the 'teat'?

Teenage years — grammar school dinners and probably too much caffeine in too many cappuccinos imbibed in the then fashionable Coffee-Bar era. The Big Mac and KFC, who appear to constitute a mandatory part of present-day teenage life, had yet to put in an appearance. Two years' National Service in Germany — definitely into heavy meat eating there.

The next thirty years I would call 'My Company Credit Card Period'. Possession of an American Express and a Diners Club card meant too many lunches, too many dinners, too much wine and too much port. My mother, being Scottish, had fed us a great many varieties of 'soup'. I promised myself, at a very early age, that for the rest of my life, if I ever got the chance to eat differently I would never let another spoonful of soup anywhere near my mouth. So whenever I was presented with a menu I always went for the more exotic starters, mostly fish or more probably, shell-fish — which was good, lots of zinc, which is very beneficial to 'willy' parts'.

It was then that I think I went wrong. Thirty years of steak and salad! And how did I like my steak cooked? Well, as the man from Texas said, "Just cut off its horns and wipe its arse" — as rare as I could get it.

Desserts, never ate puddings — too many milk puddings when young — rice, semolina and that awful tapioca, dreadful stuff with a "No, you won't go out to play unless you eat it all". So it was the cheese board. In thirty years I must have tried practically every cheese from every country in Europe — my favourite being the Italian Dolcelatte squashed onto a stick of celery — and it still is.

So there you have it, a bit like the 'parson's egg, good in parts'. My diet over the last fifteen years has been much better. I'm into the life of the five 'Fs' sorry, four 'Fs' — Fish, Fur, Feathers and Fruit with plenty of raw vegetables and salads. I eat very little meat, the odd Sunday roast and I rue the day that I gave up soups —all those years missing out on some of the greatest dishes in the world. What a waste. Overall, looking back, I thought I was eating sensibly. It was all a little too little and a lot too late, I'm afraid.

If I had my time over again, what would I change? What could I change?

Put very simply — my search for knowledge and I don't mean to sound pretentious but if I'd had the slightest inkling that, by the turn of the century, 60 per cent, yes 60 per cent of all males in the UK, over the age of forty would have an enlarged prostate — and that I would be one of them — which could lead on to impotency, then yes I would have done something about it.

I would have drunk more water daily. I would have maintained a diet, which included more raw vegetables, fruit, rice, nuts and seeds. I would have cut down on the eating of meat and refined carbohydrates, drinking gallons of coffee per day, and definitely stopped smoking sooner than I did.

If I had known that there were natural products that promoted good health in the male genital area then I would have taken them. Such products as Saw Palmetto, derived from the berries of a palm tree, lycopene found in tomato sauces, teas made from the common-or-garden stinging nettle, or Pygeum from the bark of a tree in Africa. We may not have known about them thirty years ago but we know now — that is some of us know now, when it is too late.

This may sound a bit way out and indeed these products are still quite expensive to buy, but the saving of £10 per day by giving up smoking, and breaking the habit of taking a couple of drinks at the bar before you go home, would buy an awful lot of first-rate supplementary tablets which would probably be beneficial to you. One thing is for sure nicotine and alcohol are not!

Today we are so much more aware of what we eat and what is in what we eat, labels have to list the contents. You may not have 'a Dad with an allotment' but you only have to walk round the 'fruit and veg' department of any supermarket to see a display that makes you want to buy a bagful of everything. There is so much beautifully packed variety. OK it might look better than it actually is. There is a great deal of exposure given to the detrimental effects of genetically modified plants and hormone-enhanced feeds for livestock, which is why I mention the supplements. It is not my intention to go into detail about these products, as there is now so much knowledge, so easily obtainable. All I would insist you do is make yourself knowledgeable, be aware of what might, no could happen to you if you don't!

CHAPTER THIRTEEN

For the next seven years I attended the Middlesex at six-monthly intervals for checkup examinations. During that time my PSA reading increased by the odd 0.2 or 0.3 — nothing of any consequence. The visits to the capital occurred in mid-summer — delightful, coffees on the pavements, lunches in the parks or by the river or, much less delightful, in mid-winter, stuffy undergrounds, cold rain slashing your face, but a chance to do some Christmas shopping.

After a couple of years there was a change in my consultant. Dr Duncan must have got so browned off with me turning up in the middle of December with a tan that she decided to up roots and fly off into the sun of the southern hemisphere. Another lady, Dr Dolor took her place, the Middlesex really do attract the best.

It was on the summer visit of '99 that I received the first jolt. I attended the normal Wednesday morning clinic in the Oncology Outpatients to find that Dr Dolor was not in attendance and I would be seen by her locum. I entered the small consulting room full of my usual confidence. The doctor was consulting my file. A file, by the way, that always looked considerably slimmer than most of the others that could be seen when checking in at reception. I took this to be a good sign. Let's keep it slim as always it sounds more healthy.

The locum looked up as I entered, he introduced himself and we conversed in general terms about my health and whether I had any recent problems. No. I was feeling fine. I asked about my PSA reading.

"Fine," he said quite casually, "a slight rise: 3.8."

That was the jolt! 3.8! I was expecting, with the small increases shown on previous visits, for it to be less than 3, but here was a rise of over a full point in just over six months! I expressed my concern.

The doctor then proceeded to explain that the PSA reading was within the limits of what was considered normal, that the increase, even as a percentage was not large enough to warrant any further testing which would not yield any further information.

He recommended 'wait and see', a term you hear quite often with prostate problems. I was not happy. I have since learnt that PSA readings of in excess of 100 are not uncommon among fellow sufferers so I could understand why he didn't react in the same 'knee-jerk alarm-bell ringing' way that I did.

I returned to the Canaries but I was still very uneasy. Within a week I had phoned Dr Dolor, I explained how I felt, and even under the interrupted, echoing sounds of a long-distance phone call she could probably read the anxiety in my voice and she agreed that we should not wait the customary six months. She would write confirming appointment times.

This duly arrived giving me different times for some tests she felt I ought to have. So it was at the beginning of September that I found myself back in the hospital buildings. On the Wednesday morning I had an ultrasound examination and this time they took half a dozen little snips from the prostate for a biopsy. The doctor warned me that I would feel a little nip as she took the sample. I did. Throughout all the visits I had made to the hospital that was the first time I had ever felt anything, and then it was no more than a nip.

The following day I was back in the Department of Nuclear Medicine — what a daunting title that is, a long way from the 'Cottage' image of yester-year. In the morning I had an injection of radio-active fluid which is given a few hours to circulate, you then return and are 'put through the hoop' where a scan of your whole body is taken. The radio-active material highlights those parts of your body where activity is taking place — the meaning of which becomes clear to only those expert consultants who know about these things. Too far away for me to contemplate. Nuclear Medicine. 'Healing-wise' I was still trying to cope with a 'hot poultice' and a dose of 'syrup of figs'!

My meeting with Dr Dolor the following Wednesday confirmed my anxieties. My PSA reading had increased, a strong sign that the cancer cells in the prostate were active again. This was confirmed by the biopsy report, but the good news was that it looked likely that they were still contained within the prostate.

Treatment — I had already had the full course of external radiotherapy back in '93 so I could have no more of that. Hormone treatment would slow down and contain the growth for a period of time only. There was an alternative. A new form of therapy was in its late stages of development, which was specially aimed at subjects like me. Patients who needed a radio-active boost. In simple terms it meant giving an internally applied 'zap' to the bad cells within the prostate thus preventing the 'zap' that the good cells get, but don't want, when receiving external radiotherapy.

The treatment would only take minutes, but it would require a few days' hospitalisation. Dr Dolor then explained how the treatment was given and advised me that it had been used with a high degree of success in other countries and at a hospital close to London. All members of the team that would perform the treatment were experienced but this would be the first time at this hospital. A 'Première', no less, and I would be centre stage. Was this to be my one 'fifteen minutes of fame'?

Dr Dolor told me I did not have to make up mind there and then but that she would send me a leaflet, giving more details of the treatment, which I could ponder over in my own time, and let her know.

The leaflet gave full details of the treatment including the possible side-effects that could occur. Briefly these were the same as those possible from external radiation and the prostatectomy, including of course the impotency. Well, I'd got that one so there was nothing to lose. It seemed a very straightforward decision to make.

I contacted Dr Dolor who said she would put the wheels in motion and aim for a treatment day in early November — just over a month away.

The treatment could only be carried out when all members of the team could be in the same hospital on the same day, at the same time, and on a day when there was an operating theatre available. With the varying work schedules of all parties involved this was not an easy task to accomplish.

It was only after several letters and telephone calls that we finally got a definite date of mid January. Sometime prior to this, when it had looked as if there might be a delay that was longer than anticipated, Dr Dolor suggested that I go on to hormone tablets, which would have the effect of slowing down any prostate activity. This I did. They came with the statutory warning of side-effects, similar to all the others but with the additions of possible irritability, bad temper and a loss of sexual drive — 'mental castration' is the strong way of putting it. All of which I got, the additional ones that is.

'Love of my...' took the full brunt, passing it off, with a shrug of the shoulders, "Exactly the same as PMT, now you know!" She was also suffering menopausal twinges as well, so you can imagine the domestic scene when things were not going right. Thankfully we were both very aware of the reasons for the flare-ups so we were mostly able to end up smiling even though our teeth may have been tightly clenched at the time.

For the week before entering hospital I stayed in a lovely house in west London with two friends whom I had met many years ago in Lanzarote. Always good company Geoff and Annie 'wined and dined' and nurtured me in a fashion I could quite readily grow accustomed to.

I was to enter the hospital late on the Sunday afternoon. The treatment would take place on the Monday and Tuesday. There being no complications I should be out on the Wednesday. A private room at the entrance to the ward had been reserved for me.

On the Wednesday prior to the weekend I saw Dr Dolor who arranged for me to be X-rayed, blood-sampled, scanned and generally 'rubber stamped' to be OK for admission and treatment.

The scan was taken in a different place but contained the similar piece of 'hoop-like' machinery, which when slid over my body concentrated mainly on the 'willy' region. I was put into the same position that I would be for the treatment, similar to that which is required when giving birth, so I was told. All the personal details, size, position, angle, depth etc. were taken and memorised by 'big brother', the computer.

I also collected from the pharmacy two envelopes of powder with explicit instructions that informed me that I had to take the contents of one, mixed with water, at 8am on the Sunday morning, and not to go too far away from a toilet, and to take the other one at around 4pm the same afternoon. 'Vacant bowels' would still appear to be the order of the day — the operation day, Monday that is. The old bag of liquid, plastic tube and nozzle seem to have gone out of the window. The powders were as equally effective, if not more so, but in a way, I missed the frantic, dramatic excitement of the old 'enema'.

On the Sunday I had a light lunch, I was surprised that I was allowed to, considering the 'vacating potion' I had taken. Geoff and Annie then chauffeured me to the hospital.

CHAPTER FOURTEEN

It must have been over twenty-five years since I had been a patient, or come to that even a visitor, in a ward in a hospital in the UK.

Time changes everything, our society evolves, nothing stands still — 'Say yes to life and move on'.

A young nurse in a blue uniform, a big smile and a warm "We wondered where you had got to" greeted me. She showed me into one of the small rooms at the entrance to the ward. Bed, bedside locker, comfortable armchair, mobile table over the bed, a TV set on top of the locker and a wash basin in the corner — not 'en suite' but two bathrooms just across the corridor.

I made myself comfortable, arranging my bedside locker, putting my wash-bag near the basin and laid the second laxative powder sachet on the table. "Ah," said the nurse, picking it up, "You have one with you. You must take it now." And she poured a glass of water and mixed the cocktail. On the ball, I thought. Impressive. She left and returned with a file on a clipboard. "I'm sorry I didn't introduce myself, my name is Geraldine and I will be looking after you while you are here. How do you like to be called, Ken or Kenneth?"

"My mother was the only one who ever called me Kenneth."

"Then Ken it will be." A glimmer of a wry smile crept into the corner of my face accompanied by a tilt of the head and a slight lift of the shoulders. This she took to be an affirmative.

She continued checking and filling in my credentials, address, telephone number, next of kin. "Religion?" she asked, then added quickly, "It doesn't matter if you don't have one."

That set me back, momentarily. Did I look like someone who didn't have a religion? I had to think about that one. True I hadn't been a practising religious person since I had left Sunday school at a very early age, but assessing where I was and what I was doing there, I suddenly felt the need to have one, a loophole, just in case.

"Presbyterian Church of Scotland. That's what my parents were," I said and then added quickly "No, no, the space on the form won't be big enough and in any case I doubt if either of us could spell it. Put down C of E."

She then gave a demonstration of the call button, light switches and TV controls. I settled down and in between a couple of visits to the 'loo' read the Sunday papers and watched a little, not a lot, of television, all with a feeling of déjà vu.

Geraldine called in to wish me "Goodnight, sleep well, I'll see you in the morning".

Shortly afterwards another nurse bustled in with a bright "Hi, Ken", introduced herself (first name) as the night nurse responsible for my care and enquired after my comfort. The atmosphere was relaxed without being carefree, warm without being cloying. I felt reasonably at ease. I slept well.

I was awoken the following morning around 7am. I showered and shaved and as my bowels had been 'vacated' some time ago, I returned to my bed but not before I had been instructed to don one of those gowns that barely reach your knees and the gaping split down the back is held together by tapes that no one ever seems to tie — it must be the most uncomfortable, confidence-destroying garment ever designed. No wonder they gave you a relaxing pre-med jab in the ward!

In due course a trolley arrived, piloted by an elderly porter and his assistant, both dressed in green cotton jackets and trousers. With practised ease they had me on the trolley, slightly inclined so as I could see where I was going, the sides up and, at a brisk pace, sailing down the corridor into the lift, down and along to the operating wing and into a room adjacent to the theatre. Bright lights, pleasant voices, a gentle hand, that is all I can remember. I went unde...

I came to in the same room, though I didn't recognise it at first. Again friendly voices like far-away angels, bright lights and a sudden fearful feeling of complete and absolute panic, I had no idea where I was. After what seemed hours but was, perhaps, barely seconds, I recognised the surroundings. The anti room of a theatre that had probably seen more dramas than all of those in Shaftesbury Avenue put together. I had appeared here many times before. I drifted off.

The next time I came round I was being lifted gently, but firmly, onto my bed. I was bolstered by pillows; I lay back and took stock. No pain, in fact no discomfort whatsoever, perhaps I was still under the effects of the anaesthetic. My legs were apart and my knees drawn up. On examination I found shaped polystyrene blocks supported them. On the lower part of my stomach, just above the 'willy', there was what appeared to feel like a large padded pillow, I took a peep under the sheet; sure enough that is exactly what it was. I quickly put the sheet back having no desire at all to explore any further. I had also noticed a plastic tube running from somewhere beyond the padded pillow to a bag hung from the side of the bed; already beginning to fill with a blood-coloured liquid. Let sleeping dogs lie, I thought, after all they had been sleeping some time now.

I had been told that a plate would be stitched securely in place between my rectum and my scrotum, and sixteen hollow needles would be strategically placed with computerised accuracy into my prostate gland, ready to receive the treatment.

This was as new to the nursing staff on the ward as it was to me, so I was the subject of some interest for a good part of the afternoon. From a nursing point of view it was important that the needles protruding from the disc should be kept in place and not to have contact with the bed. I therefore had to be propped up from the very small of my back so that my pelvis pointed upwards, and I would have to maintain this position until the following afternoon.

At around 4pm a trolley arrived pushed by two young men. In order to get the trolley into the room the bed had to be moved to the side. In order to get me onto the trolley either the bed had to be raised, or the trolley lowered, and the brakes applied to both 'vehicles' before any moving of bodies were to be attempted.

Neither of the two trolley pushers seemed able to accomplish any of these functions, but with a little help from Geraldine and her colleagues, I was eventually propped onto the trolley and whisked away.

Whatever my two 'pushers' lacked in mechanical training they certainly made up for in patient/porter relationships. Their youthful exuberance was quite catching with their deft, swift manoeuvring of the trolley and the ribald comments between themselves and anyone they knew who happened to pass, was very entertaining. I arrived at my destination in high spirits. That terminal being the basement beneath the Oncology Clinic, down the ramp and into a room that must have been quite close to my old adversary 'Buzz 22'.

I was handed over to the staff of the radiotherapy centre. If this were the 'Première' of this type of treatment — Brachytherapy, to give it its correct name — then there was no sign of first night nerves. Everything was handled in a calm, very professional manner.

I was placed on a table; my hips and legs were put into position. I was then slid under what was, amongst other things no doubt, a mobile TV camera. Nearby sat, menacingly, a piece of machinery that resembled an old-fashioned cannon, with a watering-can rose on the end of the nozzle. I was later to learn that the cost of all the equipment used in this treatment was in excess of £1,500,000.

If I turned my head to the right I could see the door to the control room and several TV monitors, one of which was displaying a picture of my genital region with my prostate resembling one of those unfortunates who didn't survive 'Custer's Last Stand' the 'Battle of the Big Horn'. (Oh, that it was!)

People came and went — People? Specialist consultants in various fields more like.

The needles were aligned to the computerised settings, and then attached by means of tubes to the nozzles of the nearby 'cannon', which was to fire the high-dose radiation into my prostate.

Everything was checked. I lay still. Everyone retired to keep the computer company. As is normal when one is exposed to radioactive material I was left 'Alone again, unnaturally'.

The equipment was set to do a dummy run, to check connections and clear passageways. The 'cannon' clicked and buzzed, clicked and buzzed… It took about six minutes; the senior radiologist came in and made an adjustment. We were 'Go minus ten, and counting'. She left, 'four, three, two, one', the machine clicked and buzzed…

If I was being bombarded with radioactive particles, as usual, I couldn't feel a thing. However twelve minutes is a long time to be with your hips on a hard block. I stifled the discomfort by imagining how the relief would feel when I was allowed to 'ease one cheek'.

The following day I was to have two more 'zapping' sessions with the nuclear 'cannon', and a hip replacement operation. No, no it was not as bad as that.

I returned to the ward where my trolley pushers, with the aid of the ever-attentive Geraldine, got me back into my bed. I made myself as comfortable as possible.

'Love of my life' had flown in from a work assignment on the continent that afternoon, and had come hot-foot straight to the hospital complete with papers, paperbacks and fruit (grapes of course). She insisted on a 'damage assessment' look at 'down there', lifted the sheet, winced and in a mock tone declared, "One hundred and eighty, you look like a dartboard". Which was quite encouraging to hear as at that particular time my chances of 'scoring' were about as good as me putting an oyster in a parking meter!

Considering the physical limitations put upon me by the 'dartboard', I slept well. The drain-bag at the foot of the bed caused me no problems, in fact, I had even forgotten it was there. I had been given a potion of some sort or another, to tighten the bowels for a day or so and the only fright that I had was when I was overcome by a huge sneeze and cough, both at the same time. Well, I thought I had fired the 'dartboard' across the room. I could have sworn I heard it hit the opposite wall. I also felt as if there was a gaping hole between my legs, which would not have been surprising considering the position I had been held in for the last couple of days. I rang for the nurse. She came. I explained. She inspected — nervous pause.

"No," she said, "everything looks fine. Just as it was before."

With a great deal of relief, I sank into the pillows.

The following morning my trolley 'pushers' dutifully turned up and with a slight improvement of technique I duly arrived back in the treatment room. The procedure was exactly the same as the previous day, except for the positioning of the 'needles' in the prostate. This took a little longer and indeed, for the first time was a little painful, made my teeth sweat a bit. But then, I had gone a whole night of some tossing and turning which may have incurred some movement and, of course, there was the 'sneeze'.

The treatment completed, I grinned like a 'Cheshire cat' as I raised my hips in the penultimate 'Lift Off' I would make off this Nuclear pad and returned to the ward.

For the first time I noticed that my room had a sort of lived-in appearance: blankets and pillows I had not used still lay on the windowsill, one or two tissues on top of the locker, a rubber glove on the floor. Little things that showed that the one-time regimental ward discipline of yesteryear had been relaxed, which, in some ways was no bad thing. Certainly the present occupant 'Ken' did not complain. I suspect that 'Mr Robson' may have said something. But then, if he had called Geraldine 'Nurse', probably he would have had no reason to. Who knows?

My lunch arrived and I could not recall what I had ordered on the day before. There was another menu on the tray on which you ticked off the meal requirement for the following day. At the bottom I noticed you could order vegetarian, halal or Kosher. I was disappointed to have missed it, as the idea of a plate of birianni with some lime pickle or a plate of salt beef, horseradish mustard and a couple of latka's would have gone down very well. As it was the food I got, like all hospital food down through the ages, was acceptable. The real marvel is that you get any at all considering the variety, the amount, and the various delivery points that have to be serviced.

The day passed quickly and just after 4pm I went down for my last 'zapping session'. It all went very smoothly, well, it was by now a 'piece of cake'. I eased both 'cheeks' off the hard pad, for the last time, with massive relief. The stitches were snipped and the 'dartboard' removed. With the best wishes of the staff of the Nuclear Medicine treatment room, who had been so supportive and caring, I returned again to the ward.

'Love of my life' was waiting. She waited a little while longer as I was wheeled in alongside my bed, and with unbounded freedom from all the encumbrances, I practically leapt on to it.

'Love of...' complained of being too hot so I suggested she opened the window, which she struggled to do —old-fashioned sash type window which wasn't working. During the struggle she accidentally knocked over a vase of flowers, sent to me by some kind friends. Crashing to the floor, the water spread everywhere. Handfuls of paper towels from the adjacent washbasin were applied to the floor with the odd one applied to the tears that had begun to flow, accompanied by some mutterings.

Not the most blissful of hospital visiting scenes.

I then said the words that have probably been the first lines to kick off many a major domestic 'ding-dong'. "Pull yourself together, it's not a catastrophe."

What I didn't know, and only found out much later, was that she had arrived some twenty minutes earlier and walked into my room only to find a well-made bed, no sign of habitation and, more significant, no sign of me! She had asked at ward reception "Where was I" only to be told they were not quite sure, but they would make a phone call.

This was disturbing enough but after the first two calls had resulted in the same negative she was a little confused and began to fret. Was one of the calls to the morgue? She hoped it had been, at least she would have known I wasn't there! Another phone call, a beaming smile, "Found him, he's on his way up."

"Pull yourself together." Whoops. "Sorry."

Dr Dolor visited me and told me that everything had gone off exceedingly well, that they would leave the drainpipe in my 'willy' until first thing the following morning, then if I could pass water satisfactorily during the day, there was no reason why I should not be out in the late afternoon.

With my seemingly inborn ability to avoid all the minor possible side-effects of most medical treatments this duly occurred. An appointment was made to see Dr Dolor in three weeks' time.

Whenever I have had to stay in London I have always been fortunate with the friends who I have there. On this occasion two of the friends, who had been of tremendous help and support throughout all of my adventures, were off to the USA for four weeks, visiting relatives. I was to house sit.

The house is situated in a mews at the top of Marylebone High Street, an area that is close to the hospital and which, of course, I knew well. We were looking forward to it and like during all good things, the time just flew. The weather was a bit 'hit or miss' but the 'hit' days were absolutely wonderful. Regents Park was awash with snowdrops and crocuses, with squirrels and pigeons that ate out of your hand and very superior looking ducks and geese who really expected to be fed with the choice pickings from a Fortnum and Mason hamper, rather that the mundane crumbs that we had to offer.

We duly presented ourselves to Dr Dolor who declared that my prostate felt fine; there were no visible scars or signs of the recent treatment, for which other patients were now being considered. My PSA had stayed at 3.8 which was as expected considering the pummelling that my prostate had received and the winding-down effect from the hormone treatment that I had only recently ceased taking.

In order that they might keep an eye on me a checkup appointment was arranged for two months' time. A goal to be scored. A result to be obtained. Or is the game over?